英会話に強くなる
英文法・英作文

Express English
Effectively!

Mark Petersen

S<small>AWAI</small> Kohsuke

JN034088

TSURUMI SHOTEN

Express English Effectively!

写真提供
p. 1 © m.Taira / PIXTA（ピクスタ）
p. 7 © y.uemura / PIXTA（ピクスタ）
p. 13 © アオサン / PIXTA（ピクスタ）
p. 19 © rjhowmanyo / PIXTA（ピクスタ）
p. 25 © Jirawatfoto / PIXTA（ピクスタ）
p. 32 © takapon / PIXTA（ピクスタ）
p. 38 © Koki / PIXTA（ピクスタ）
p. 44 © VisionLabs / PIXTA（ピクスタ）
p. 51 © 花火 / PIXTA（ピクスタ）
p. 57 © Hakase / PIXTA（ピクスタ）
p. 63 © K.Konta / PIXTA（ピクスタ）
p. 69 © おおたま / PIXTA（ピクスタ）
p. 76 © artswai / PIXTA（ピクスタ）
p. 83 © PicStyle / PIXTA（ピクスタ）
p. 89 © ゆえこ / PIXTA（ピクスタ）

自習用音声について

本書の自習用音声は以下よりダウンロードできます。予習，復習に
ご利用ください。
（2024 年 4 月 1 日開始予定）

http://www.otowatsurumi.com/00585/

URL はブラウザのアドレスバーに直接入力して下さい。

音声の記号とトラック番号について

 ～ 　自習用音声のトラック番号です。

 ～ 　教授用 CD のトラック番号です。

※録音された音声は，アメリカ人男性とイギリス人女性によるものです。

まえがき

　高校での英語学習や受験勉強が終わって大学生となったみなさんは，話すためのトレーニングに本格的に取り組みたいという意欲をお持ちのことでしょう。

　英語を話すということは，熟達度に応じて個人差はあると思いますが，頭の中で英作文したものを口に出す，ということになるのが普通です。つまり「英作文力 ≒ 英語の発信力」なのです。そして英作文ができるためには次の2つの力が求められます。

　① 正しい規則に従って，文の適切な枠組みを構築できる。
　② その枠組みの中に，伝えたい意味がきちんと伝えられるように語彙を埋め込むことができる。

　文というのは，英文に限らず，規則に厳しく縛られながら存在しています。むやみに単語だけを連ねても，表現したい意味の文にはなりません。そしてその規則こそが，英文法なのです

　本書は，英文を生み出す際に，特に有効な15の文法事項を学ぶためのものです。各章は4部構成ですが，まずは **1** で，大学生の日常を垣間見ながら，その章で学ぶ項目に触れます。次に **2** で，教養につながるトピックを読みながら，他の例も見ていきます。**3** はその章で扱う文法事項の解説です。最後に **4** で英作文に挑みます。

　本書は密度を徹底的に高めていますので，正面から取り組むことにより，みなさんの英作文力，英会話力が大きく進歩することを約束できます。どうぞ大きな期待とともにお付き合いください

2023年　秋

マーク・ピーターセン
澤井 康佑

Contents

CHAPTER 1
that 節を使いこなす

think that ~, explain to … that ~, suggest that ~ など，「動詞＋that 節」を用いれば，「説明」「提案」などが可能になる。思考と感情の機微を表現する用法を学んでみよう。

1 **Opening Dialogue** ▷▷▷▷▷▷ 野球部に入るべきか

★下線を引いた文に注意し，表現を覚えよう

Satomi: Are you really not going to join the university baseball team?

Shota: That's right.

Satomi: But they scouted you, didn't they? They want you, don't they, knowing how you played in high school?

Shota: I've decided that just playing through high school was enough for me. 5

Satomi: Is there something else you want to do?

Shota: Actually, I want to become a CPA. On a university athletic team, I'd never be able to get the time I need to study for the qualifying exam. My parents say that they want me to keep playing baseball, though.

Satomi: I feel the same way. I'd love to see you play at Jingu Stadium. 10

Shota: But I want to work part-time, too, and it would be impossible to do all of those things.

Satomi: What about if you limited how often you went to practice?

Shota: That's actually what the team captain says. He says that I could come to practices whenever I wanted to. He'd leave it all up to me. 15

Satomi: If that's the case, I think that you ought to join the team.

Shota: That wouldn't be fair to the other players. They'll all have to practice six days a week. It'd be too self-centered of me just to go whenever I wanted to.

Satomi: I guess that's true. But if the captain himself thinks that it's okay, I don't imagine that the other players would have any objections. 20

Shota: If true, that would be nice—the best possible situation. If it wouldn't create any relationship problems, I would, in fact, really like to join the team.

Satomi: <u>I believe that a person like you would surely get along well with all the others.</u> You have the talent—it would be a shame if you quit baseball now. <u>I'm sure that you could be a college baseball star.</u>

Shota: Thanks. <u>I guess that I'll give it a try.</u> And I'll try to think a little more positively from now on, too.

25

NOTES ————

7 **CPA** 「公認会計士」certified public accountant の略。／ 8 **qualifying exam**「資格検定試験, 資格認定試験」／ 15 **leave ~ all up to** …「~をすべて…にまかせる」

2 *Understanding More Variations*

次の英文を読み，（　　　）内の和訳を参考に，英単語を並べ替えてみよう。なお，文頭に置かれる語は大文字で始めてください。

Dialogue A ゴミを持ちかえったら犯罪です

A: Did you know it's a crime to take possession of someone's thrown-away trash?

B: Really? That's unbelievable.

A: It's true. I'd been using a bicycle that somebody living in my condominium had abandoned, but when I told a police officer about it yesterday, she said that that was a crime and (1. その自転車を引き渡すよう要求してきたんだ).

B: You're right. It *is* true. An Internet check here shows that it seems to be a violation of Article 254 of the Penal Code.

1. (to / turn / her / demanded / the bicycle / that / I / over)

···

● **NOTES**
condominium「分譲アパート（の一室）。いわゆる日本のマンションはこれにあたる」／**Penal Code**「刑法」

Dialogue B 芸術作品に対する鑑識眼

A: There are a lot of museums—natural history museums, art museums—in the Metropolitan area, but my students rarely visit any.

B: It's the same with my students. They tend to show interest only in things they've made themselves.

A: (2. 私は彼らに繰り返し伝えている) by viewing a large number of superb works they will refine the discernment in their eye for art.

B: I always stress the same thing. And also that when they are creating things themselves, a discerning eye will be crucial to their success.

2. (that / I / them / over and over / tell)

....

● **NOTES**
discernment「鑑識眼，識別力」

Dialogue C 税について知ろう！

A: I'm a tax accountant, but my son doesn't even know the rudiments of taxation.

B: Why should that be a problem? He *is*, after all, still just a college student.

A: Well, I would like him to know just a little about it. The other day, (3. 税には 2 種類あるのだということを彼に説明してやったよ), national taxes and local taxes.

3. (explained / are / him / I / taxes / that / there / two types of / to)

....

● **NOTES**
tax accountant「税理士」 ／ **rudiment**「基礎，初歩，基本」

Dialogue D 長崎に生まれてよかった

A: During the summer vacation, I traveled to Nagasaki, which you had recommended to me.

B: How was it?

A: Well, for one thing, the night view of the port was wonderful.

B: I'm glad you thought so. It's nice to hear good things said about my home town. I think Nagasaki Port offers the most beautiful night view in Japan. (4. 私は自分が長崎生まれであることを誇りに思っているんだ).

4. (I / that / feel / born / Nagasaki / was / I / in / proud)

....

3 Focus on Grammar

文法を理解しよう

★ 動詞＋（前置詞）＋（名詞）＋that 節／形容詞＋that 節

Q&A

Q1 I demanded that he apologized to me. という文はどこが誤りか。

Q2 〈SV＋that 節〉という構造の文に，伝達相手（これを X とする）を加える場合，どのような形になるか。

Q3 〈SV＋X＋that 節〉の X を主語にして書き換えた文はどのような型になるか。

Q4 that 節が後続する形容詞にはどのようなものがあるか。

Q5 上記の that は省略が可能か。

A1 「提案」「要求」「命令」などの意味をもつ動詞（demand, suggest, insist, propose, order など）に続く that 節内においては，述語を原形または〈should＋原形〉にする。

A2 主に〈SV＋X＋that 節〉という型になる場合と，〈SV＋to X＋that 節〉という型になる場合の 2 つに分かれる。いずれになるかは動詞による。

A3 〈S be V（過去分詞形）＋that 節 (by ~)〉という型になる。by 以下は省略されることも多い。

A4 主に「①感情」「②人の性格・性質，境遇」「③対象をもつもの」の 3 つに分かれる。①は glad, sad, surprised など。②は mad, crazy, lucky, unlucky など。③は sure（〜を確信している），proud（〜を誇りに思う）のようなもの。③の形容詞は他動詞と同じように対象をもつ。

A5 可能。いずれも頻繁に省略される。

例文

① We insisted that she should come to the party.

② She proposed that we start at seven.

③ I suggested to him that he join the basketball team.

④ She proposed to me that we go out for a walk.

⑤ My father taught me that I must always keep my word.

⑥ Her smile convinced us that she was happy.

⑦ I was sad that my adventure was over.

⑧ You are lucky that your son did not get drafted.

⑨ Everyone thinks he is crazy that he would leave his wife to do such a thing.

⑩ They are now certain that there was no other choice.

⑪ I believe he is still alive.

⑫ I'm sure he can solve this problem.

⑬ We were told that he was alive.

解説

■ ①②　insist は「主張する」，propose は「提案する」という意味なので，that 節内の述語が①では〈should＋原形〉，②では〈原形〉になっている。

■ ③④⑤⑥　伝達相手が加わった形。③，④は〈SV＋to X＋that 節〉の型，⑤，⑥は〈SV＋X＋that 節〉の型。

■ ⑦⑧⑨⑩　〈形容詞＋that 節〉が含まれる文。⑦の sad は「感情」，⑧の lucky は「人の境遇」，⑨の crazy は「人の性格・性質」，⑩の certain は「対象をもつもの」。なお⑨の thinks の後ろには that が省略されている。

■ ⑪⑫　that の省略が見られる文。

■ ⑬　〈S be V（過去分詞形）＋that 節〉の型の文。

4 Exercises

次の文を指定された語数で英訳しましょう。（　　　　）内で示されている語は必要に応じて，形を変えたうえで用いてください。

① 彼らは彼女が潔白だと結論づけた。（6 語／ conclude, innocent）

....

② 彼女は私たちが彼女の家で一緒に住むことを提案した。（9 語／ suggest）

....

③ 彼は私にあまりにも忙しいことを説明した。（9 語）

....

④ その警官は私たちにその公園は閉鎖されていると告げた。（9 語／ inform）

....

⑤ 私は彼に助けてあげることを約束した。(8 語／ promise)

⑥ 私たちは彼が成功するはずだと確信している。(7 語／ sure)

⑦ 私たちは彼がうちの会社を去らなければならないことが悲しかった。(10 語／ sad)

⑧ 私たちは自分の母語が英語でなく不幸だ。(10 語／ unlucky, tongue)

⑨ 私はあなたが自分の仕事に満足していないことを十分に理解できる。(12 語／ fully)

⑩ 私は自分の声はラジオ向きではないと妻から言われた。(14 語／ fit) ※ radio で文を終える

CHAPTER 2
何かをしてもらう，何かをさせるには

動詞と to 不定詞の間に（代）名詞を挟む形，つまり，ask me to, want us to などを使えば，「命令」「要求」「依頼」「希望」などの簡潔な表現を作ることができる。基本動詞の意味も再確認しながら様々な用法を考えたい。

1 Opening Dialogue ▷▷▷▷▷▷ 自分の車を買いたいんだけれど…

★ 下線を引いた文に注意し，表現を覚えよう

Maki: Hi! You're coming to school by bike again! You got it fixed?

Masashi: Yeah. I got my father to fix it.

Maki: Your father is quite the handyman, isn't he?

Masashi: He's always repaired all sorts of things for us. But actually I'd rather commute by motorcycle. With a motorcycle, it would be a lot easier, and I could go on touring trips, too. The problem is, though, that I don't have a license. 5

Maki: Why don't you just get one?

Masashi: It's the money. I work part-time, but I spend what I make on things like clothes or a new watch, and I never manage to save anything. You've got a driver's license, haven't you? 10

Maki: I do, and I do a lot of driving by car.

Masashi: That must be nice.

Maki: Yes, but since I got my license, my mother has been taking advantage of me. Whenever she wants to go out for shopping, she always asks me to take her in our car. 15

Masashi: I guess she must be quite happy about being able to do that now.

Maki: *Very* happy. She says it makes her shopping so much easier. But to me it's a real bother.

Masashi: C'mon, I think that it's a fine way to try to repay a mother for all that she's done for you so far in life. 20

Maki: Well, I do get to use the family car, so I guess I should try to show a little gratitude. But I really *would* like a car of my own. Ours is a subcompact, and I'd like something a bit cooler. The fact is, though, I can't buy one.

Masashi: So, you've got a money problem, too?

Maki: No, I've saved up enough to buy a used car. 25

Masashi: Then why don't you just do that?

Maki: <u>My father won't allow me to buy one.</u> He says that one car is enough for us and that another would be a waste of money.

Masashi: Well, it's your own money that we're talking about. Why not use it however you want? 30

Maki: I'd like to do that, but I have respect for my father. Also, I think his argument does make sense, and I'm going to go along with it for now.

NOTES —————

5 **commute**「通勤・通学する」／ 22 **gratitude**「感謝の気持ち」／ 22 **subcompact**「小型自動車」／ 32 **go along with** ~「~に従う，賛成する」

2 *Understanding More Variations*

次の英文を読み，（　　　）内の和訳を参考に，英単語を並べ替えてみよう。なお，文頭に置かれる語は大文字で始めてください。

Dialogue A クラシックに詳しいわけ

A: I hear you really know a lot about classical music.

B: When I was little, (1. 母が無理やりバロック音楽や古典派の音楽をたくさん私に聴かせたんだ)。

A: Baroque is from composers like Bach, right?

B: That's right—Bach, Handel, Vivaldi. The Classical period was later, with greats like Mozart and Beethoven.

1. (to / me / a lot of / to / forced / my mother / Baroque and Classical period music / listen)

....

Dialogue B saké は英語です

A: The number of Japanese rice wine aficionados abroad seems to be on the increase.

B: And the term "saké" has already become established as a word in English. Try looking it up in an English-Japanese dictionary.

A: Here it is! Personally, (2. 私は日本酒が世界でよりいっそう広く受け入れられればと願っているんだ). I hope that it eventually achieves worldwide recognition, that it gains the same status as that of wine from grapes.

2. (widely / I / saké / more / appreciated / want / to / be even)

....

● NOTES
aficionado「愛好者，マニア」／ **Penal Code**「刑法」

Dialogue C 歴史的事実への評価は変わる

A: Historical facts have a way of being reevaluated, don't they.

B: They certainly do. Take the Japanese Navy's surprise attack on Pearl Harbor, for instance. In the past, it was generally seen as having been dastardly and underhanded, but that view has been changing lately.

A: It certainly has. (3. 今は多くの人が日本が攻撃するよう仕向けられたって考えてるんだ) by U.S. President Franklin Roosevelt.

3. (was / attack / many / people / that / induced / make / now think / to / Japan / the)

....

● NOTES
reevaluate「再評価する」／ **dastardly**「卑怯な，卑劣な」／ **underhanded**「不正の，こそこそした」

3 Focus on Grammar

文法を理解しよう

★動詞＋名詞＋ to do

Q&A

Q1 「XがYに対して，何かすることを強制する」ということを動詞 force を用いて述べる場合，〈S force that 節〉の型で表現することは可能か。たとえば，He often forces that she washes his car. というような文は正しいか。

Q2 〈S V O to do〉の型で用いられる動詞は，どのような意味をもつものが多いか。

Q3 A2 のグループの動詞の後ろに，受動態の文を置く場合，文全体の型はどうなるか。

Q4 get をこの型で用いた場合，どのような意味になるか。

Q5 〈S V O to do〉の型が受動態になると，どのような型になるか。

A1 不可能。force は〈SVO to do〉の型を用いる。

A2 主に次のような意味をもつ動詞が中心。

① 「命令する」「要求する」「依頼する」「説得する」「励ます」のように，他者に行動を促すという意味をもつもの。具体例は order, tell, ask, persuade, encourage など。

② 促さないまでも，「許可をする」「放置する」という意味をもつもの。具体例は permit, allow など

③ 「望む」「期待する」という意味をもつもの。具体例は want, expect など。

A3 〈SVO to be done（過去分詞形）〉という型になる。

A4 「S は O に〜<u>してもらう</u>」「S は O に〜<u>させる</u>」という意味になる。

A5 〈S be V（過去分詞形）to do（by 〜）〉という型になる。by 以下は省略されることも多い。

例文

① He ordered us to stay at home and not to go out at all.

② He persuaded me to accept his offer.

③ My mother never allows me to wear jeans.

④ If you go to college, we will expect you to study as hard as possible.

⑤ We expect him to arrive at 9:00.

⑥ My father taught me to ride a bike.

⑦ No one ever expected him to be awarded a special prize.

⑧ The government allowed her to be released from prison.

⑨ I got my father to drive me to the station.

⑩ I got my secretary to copy the document.

⑪ We were told to wait outside.

⑫ I was asked by my boss to file past records.

解説

- ①② order は「命令する」，persuade は「説得して納得させる」の意味。

- ③ allow は「許可する」の意味。

- ④⑤ expect は心に思うだけの行為。④のように「（当然のこととして）期待する」の意味である場合と，⑤のように「予期する」「予測する」の意味があることに注意。

- ⑥ 〈teach O that 節〉は「O に that 節の内容を教える」という意味であり，いわば"知識の伝達"だが，⑥のような〈teach O to do〉の場合は，「O が～できるように教え込む」という意味であり，いわば"技術の伝授"。意味が異なることに注意。

- ⑦⑧ 〈SVO to be done（過去分詞形）〉の型の文。SV の後ろに受動態の文が埋め込まれている例。

- ⑨⑩ 〈SVO to do〉の型の文で，V に get が用いられたもの。S と O の関係によって，「してもらう」の意味にも，「させる」の意味にもなりうる。⑨は O が父親なので「してもらう」。⑩は目下の秘書なので「させる」。ただし，この場合も「してもらう」と考えても問題はない。

- ⑪⑫ 〈SVO to do〉の受動態である，〈S be V（過去分詞形）to do（by ～）〉の型の文。⑫では by ～ の情報が，V と to の間に置かれている。to 不定詞句が長い場合，しばしばこのような形になる。

4 Exercises

次の文を指定された語数で英訳しましょう。（　　　　）内で示されている語は必要に応じて，形を変えたうえで用いてください。

① 私は夫に喫煙をやめてもらった。（7 語／ get）

....

② 私たちはあなたにここにいてほしい。（6 語／ want）

....

③ 私は彼に決して私のもとを去らないようお願いした。(7 語／ ask)

………………………………………………………………………………………………

④ 母は私が 1 人で海外に行くのを許さなかった。(9 語／ allow)

………………………………………………………………………………………………

⑤ 私は父から車を洗うよう言われた。(10 語／ tell)

………………………………………………………………………………………………

⑥ 私たちは黙っているよう命じられた。(6 語／ order)

………………………………………………………………………………………………

⑦ 私は無理やりクラスの前で歌わされた。(10 語／ force)

………………………………………………………………………………………………

⑧ 私の父は，私に大学院に進むよう励ましてくれた。(9 語)

………………………………………………………………………………………………

⑨ 我々はその美術館の中で写真を撮ることは許してもらえなかった。(11 語)

………………………………………………………………………………………………

⑩ 私たちは公の場ではスペイン語を話さないよう要請された。(10 語／ areas)

………………………………………………………………………………………………

CHAPTER 3

動詞が2つある文っておかしくないですか？

hear, see などいわゆる知覚動詞, make, let, have などの使役動詞は，後ろに動詞の原形を伴うため，英語学習者は違和感を覚えることも少なくない。この用法をマスターして，英語的な感覚も身につけたい。

1 Opening Dialogue ▷▷▷▷▷▷ 地震に負けない助け合いの心

★下線を引いた文に注意し，表現を覚えよう

Koji: That earthquake yesterday was terrible.

Rie: It really was. They said it was a magnitude five.

Koji: I was taking a nap at home and jumped right out of bed. What were you doing?

Rie: I was shopping at a neighborhood convenience store. Things started falling off ₅ shelves all over, and it was really scary. <u>I heard some of the customers scream.</u>

Koji: That was no time to be shopping!

Rie: Everybody ran outside.

Koji: You, too?

Rie: Sure. I got right out. <u>And from there I could see people run out of other stores, ₁₀ too.</u>

Koji: I guess it's just a knee-jerk reaction for people to want to get out of buildings right away.

Rie: But then I thought about the store clerks. <u>I went back in and helped them put things back on the shelves.</u> ₁₅

Koji: How nice of you! How long did it take?

Rie: It took us about 20 minutes to get everything back in place.

Koji: Did they appreciate your help?

Rie: They definitely did. They seemed a little apologetic, but they were also very grateful. As a reward, the manager gave me a sweet bean-paste bun and a meat ₂₀ bun.

Koji: That was nice.

Rie: The manager was a really cool person, and I had our picture taken together.

Koji: <u>Let me see it.</u>

Rie: Sure. Here it is. 25

Koji: Wow! What a cool looking manager! And you both have wonderful smiles on your faces. Does that bag have the buns in it?

Rie: Right. I was hungry and ate them as soon as I got home. They tasted all the better because they had been presents.

Koji: That was great—a good deed and a nice reward for it, too. 30

NOTES —————

12 **knee-jerk**「反射的な」 ／ 19 **apologetic**「申し訳なさそうな」 ／ 20 **bean-paste bun**「あんまん」 ／ 28– **all the better because ~**「～であるからなおさら良い」

2 **Understanding More Variations**

次の英文を読み，（　　　）内の和訳を参考に，英単語を並べ替えてみよう。なお，文頭に置かれる語は大文字で始めてください。

Dialogue A 小説は文体が大事

A: Last week, (1. 自分が書いた短編小説を親父に読んでもらったんだ).

B: Your father works in the literary department of a publishing company, doesn't he? What did he think of the story?

A: He said that the plot was interesting but that my writing style was immature. He said that an important key to success for a writer of fiction was to create and maintain a solid style of one's own.

B: Well, it *isn't* very pleasant to read writing that's stylistically poor, is it? Even when that writing is a piece of nonfiction.

1. (written / I / had / read / I / a short story / my father / had)

....

● **NOTES**

department「部門，課」 ／ **immature**「未熟な，成長しきっていない」 ／ **maintain**「維持する，保つ」

Dialogue B　環境保護のために何ができるか

A: I saw a report that showed the area of rainforest on the island of Borneo to be disappearing at an alarmingly fast rate.

B: (2. この種のニュースを聞くと [that 以下のことを] 思わざるを得ない) that there is nothing I myself can do to help preserve the earth's natural environment.

A: But we can't just say it's all the fault of other people, can we?

B: No, we can't—many of Japan's economic activities are, in fact, part of the cause of tropical-rainforest loss.

2.（ me / that / kind / feel / of / news / makes ）

....

● **NOTES**
preserve「保護する，保存する」

Dialogue C　窓から入ってきたものは

A: Last night, I had an unpleasant surprise. (3. 目が覚めて，近くで何かが動くのに気づいたんだ). What do you think it was?

B: A mouse?

A: No. It was a bat! It seems to have slipped in through the gap in a window I had left ajar. It was really creepy, but I was able to catch it with a fishing net and set it free outside.

3.（ near / something / I / woke / and / noticed / me / move / up ）

....

● **NOTES**
ajar「少し開いている」／ **creepy**「ぞっとさせる，気味が悪い」

3 Focus on Grammar

文法を理解しよう

★ 動詞＋名詞＋ do

Q&A

> **Q1** 「XがYに対して，何かすることを強制する」という内容を述べるのに，force, compel の 2 語を用いる場合と make を用いる場合で，文全体の型はどのように異なるか。
>
> **Q2** 「XがYに対して，何かをすることを許す」という内容を述べるのに，allow, permit の 2 語を用いる場合と let を用いる場合で，文全体の型はどのように異なるか。
>
> **Q3** 〈SV 名詞 do（原形）〉の型で用いられる動詞の代表例として，make, let の他にどのようなものがあるか。
>
> **Q4** 〈SVO do〉の型が受動態になると，どのような型になるか。

A1 force, compel は〈SVO to do〉の型で用いられるが，make は〈SVO do〉の型で用いられる。つまり O の後ろの動詞は原形となる。

A2 allow, permit は〈SVO to do〉の型で用いられるが，let は〈SVO do〉の型で用いられる。

A3 知覚動詞（「見る」「聞く」「感じる」などの意味をもつもの），have（〜させる，〜してもらう，〜される），help など。ただし help は〈SVO to do〉の型でも用いられる。

A4 〈S be V（過去分詞形）to do（by 〜）〉という型になる。to が現れることに注意（by 以下は省略されることも多い）。ただし，知覚動詞を用いる場合，この型よりも次章で扱う〈S be V（過去分詞形）doing（by 〜）〉という型で用いられることが多い。

例文

① My father made me swim in the river.

② This shirt will make you look younger.

③ He didn't let me use his car.

④ Why did he let his car get that dirty?

⑤ This tool lets you draw parallel lines.

⑥ I watched a stray dog enter the house.

⑦ He felt something creep on his face.

⑧ That strict teacher had her rewrite her essay six times.

⑨ I had my mother knit this sweater for you.

⑩ He helped me (to) push my car.

⑪ The prisoner was heard to exclaim "Enough!"

⑫ He was seen to enter her apartment.

解説

■ ①② ともに〈S make O do〉の型だが，①の make は「強制」の意味。②の文は「このシャツはあなたがより若く見える状態を作り出すでしょう（→このシャツを着ればあなたはより若く見えるでしょう）」という意味であり，make に「強制」のニュアンスはない。

■ ③④⑤ ③の let は「許可する」，④は「放置する」，⑤は「可能にする」「～の状態を作り出す」という意味。let は「許可する」「許す」という意味だけではないことに注意。

■ ⑥⑦ 〈S 知覚動詞 O do〉の型の文。

■ ⑧⑨ 〈S had O do〉の型の文。第 2 章で扱った〈S get O to do〉とほとんど同様に，主に「～させる」「～してもらう」と訳すが，以下のような例もある。
She had her husband die on her last year.（彼女は去年，夫に死なれた）

■ ⑩ help が用いられた場合は，O の直後に to が現れることもある。

■ ⑪⑫ 〈SVO to do〉の型の受動態である，〈S be V（過去分詞形）to do〉の型の文。

4 Exercises

次の文を指定された語数で英訳しましょう。（　　　　）内で示されている語は必要に応じて，形を変えたうえで用いてください。

① 私は妻が助けを求めて叫ぶのが聞こえなかったのです。（8 語／ cry, for）

....

② 私たちは一頭のイルカが自分たちのボートの下で泳ぐのを観察していた。（8 語／ watch）

....

③ 彼がその部屋を出るのに気づきましたか？（7 語／ leave）

....

④ どうやったら私は彼女が夢を達成するのを助けられるだろうか？（8語／achieve）

....

⑤ 私をあなたの秘書にしてください。（5語）

....

⑥ 彼を黙らせろ！（4語）

....

⑦ 彼のジョークは私たちを笑わせた。（5語）

....

⑧ 私たちは全速力で航行している船から男の人が落ちるのを見た。（12語）

....

⑨ 私は自分の頬が火照るのを感じた。（6語）

....

⑩ 彼女はボトルから直接ワインを飲むのを見られた。（10語）

....

CHAPTER 4
「ネコが鳩を捕まえているのを見た」と言えますか？

hear, see などのいわゆる知覚動詞，have などの使役動詞，そして leave などの動詞が，どのように現在分詞・過去分詞と組み合わされるのか考えてみよう。この用法もまた，英語的な感覚にあふれた表現を作り出す。

1 Opening Dialogue ▷▷▷▷▷ ネコが戯れるキャンパスの芝生の上で…

★下線を引いた文に注意し，表現を覚えよう

Takashi: This time of year here on campus, it feels good just to lie down on the grass, stretched out like this. Hey! I just saw two cats. This school really has a lot of cats living on the grounds, doesn't it? I wonder how many there are.

Reiko: I don't know, but there must be at least ten. A day never goes by without my seeing one. But these campus cats never cozy up to students, do they? They're 5 not at all like pet cats. They seem just like wild animals.

Takashi: Life is a real struggle for stray cats. <u>Not long ago, I saw a black cat catching a pigeon.</u>

Reiko: Wow! I'd like to have seen that.

Takashi: That cat was a real hunter. 10

Reiko: You should have got pictures or video with your smartphone.

Takashi: I couldn't. It all happened too fast for that. I just wish I could have seen the whole thing from beginning to end.

Reiko: From where it first crept up toward its prey?

Takashi: That's right. 15

Reiko: Anyway, how about if you, Satoshi, and I go out for drinks tonight?

Takashi: I wouldn't invite Satoshi out tonight.

Reiko: Why not?

Takashi: I ran into him a short time ago and found out that <u>he had his bag stolen this morning at a coffee shop</u>. It seems his wallet was in it, too. I don't think he'd be 20 able to pay his share for any drinks today.

Reiko: That's terrible. But isn't it awfully rare for things to be stolen at coffee shops in Japan?

Takashi: Actually, it seems to be getting more common lately. <u>The other day, at my regular coffee shop, I saw an employee pasting up a notice warning customers to</u> 25 <u>beware of theft.</u>

Reiko: I go to coffee shops a lot—I guess I ought to start being a little more careful.

Takashi: You should. Now, how about just the two of us going someplace for a drink?

Reiko: Let's do that. And we can start now by going to the station. 30

Takashi: Okay.

NOTES

5 **cozy up**「親しくなろうとする，擦り寄る」/ 7 **stray cat**「野良猫」/ 14 **crept up** → creep up「忍び寄る，こっそり近づく」/ 26 **beware of ~**「～に注意する，気をつける」

2 Understanding More Variations

次の英文を読み，（　　　）内の和訳を参考に，英単語を並べ替えてみよう。なお，文頭に置かれる語は大文字で始めてください。

Dialogue A　名作の朗読を聴く

A: A while ago, (1. 泉鏡花の短編「高野聖」を朗読されるのを聞いたんだ) on YouTube.

B: YouTube has things like that, too?

A: Yes, and listening to a piece of writing is a very different experience from reading one.

B: That's interesting. I'll see if I can find a reading of something by Tanizaki Jun'ichirō—he's one of my favorites.

1. (by / I / an actor / short story "Kōya Hijiri" / Izumi Kyōka's / read / heard)

....

Dialogue B　古典を読み友を待つ

A: (2. 待たせてごめん). I'm half an hour late!

B: Don't worry about it. I've been reading an interesting book.

A: What book is it?

B: It's the autobiography of Edward Gibbon, the famous 18th century English historian. His greatest work, *The History of the Decline and Fall of the Roman Empire*, is a monumental classic, and it's still read today.

2. (you / waiting / sorry / to / kept / have)

....

● **NOTES**
monumental「巨大な」／ **classic**「不朽の作品」

Dialogue C　ソクラテスよりはまし

A: (3. 靴ひもがほどけたままにするなよ). It looks terrible.
B: Why? They say Socrates went barefoot. At least it's not as bad as that.
A: You mean Socrates the ancient Greek philosopher? Is that story true?
B: I don't know, but I *do* seem to remember reading it somewhere.

3. (shoelaces / untied / don't / your / leave)

....

Dialogue D　誰かレポートのチェックお願いします

A: Have you finished that paper you were having trouble with?
B: Yes, somehow. But I've never taken a course in development economics before, and I'm not at all confident about what I've written.
A: (4. 誰かにチェックしてもらったら)?
B: I'd like to do that, but I can't find anybody that seems right for the job.

4. (it / don't / somebody / have / you / checked / why / by)

....

● **NOTES**
development economics「開発経済学」

3 Focus on Grammar

文法を理解しよう

★動詞＋名詞＋分詞

Q&A

Q1 知覚動詞の後ろに，進行形の文内容を置く場合は，文全体はどのような型になるか。

Q2 第3章で扱った〈知覚動詞＋O＋do〉と〈知覚動詞＋O＋doing〉では，どのような意味の違いがあるか。

Q3 知覚動詞の後ろに受動態の文内容を置く場合は，文全体はどのような型になるか。

Q4 〈SVO doing〉〈SVO done〉の型で用いられる動詞の代表例として，知覚動詞の他にどのようなものがあるか。

Q5 〈SVO doing〉の型が受動態になると，どのような型になるか。

A1 〈SVO doing（現在分詞）〉という型になる。be動詞を省いたうえで置くことに注意。

A2 前者が「何かを少なくとも一瞬見た／聞いた／感じた」というニュアンスになるのに対して，後者はSVの後ろに置かれている文の元の形が進行形であるだけに，「何かをある程度の時間で見ていた／聞いていた／感じていた」というニュアンスになり，前者よりも臨場感が幾分かある。

A3 〈SVO done（過去分詞形）〉という型になる。ここでもbe動詞を省く。

A4 keep, leave, have, get など。

A5 〈S be V（過去分詞形）doing (by ~)〉という型になる。by は省略されることも多い。

例文

① She watched him solving a difficult puzzle.

② I noticed an ant carrying a crumb of bread.

③ They kept me waiting.

④ They left their children playing in the playground

⑤ The king kept his arms crossed at his waist.

⑥ I left the door unlocked when I went out.

⑦ I had my hair cut by my mother.

⑧ I got new air-conditioning installed in the living room.

⑨ He had his house destroyed in a flood.

⑩ I got the computer started.

⑪ She got the job done before the end of the week.

⑫ Have the work finished by seven.

⑬ He got his leg broken.

⑭ He was noticed breaking open the window.

解説

■ ①② 〈SVO doing（現在分詞）〉の型で，V が知覚動詞である例。

■ ③④ 〈SVO doing（現在分詞）〉の型で，V が keep, leave である例。いずれも「しておいた」と訳せる語だが，keep は「保っておく」，leave は「放置しておく」のニュアンス。

■ ⑤⑥ 〈SVO done（過去分詞形）〉の型で，V が keep, leave であるもの。訳，ニュアンスの違いは③，④の場合と同じ。

■ ⑦⑧⑨⑩⑪⑫⑬ 〈SVO done（過去分詞形）〉の型で，V が get, have であるもの。これらの動詞がこの型で用いられた場合は，文脈によって「してもらう」「させる」「される」「されてしまう」「する」「してしまう」などと訳し分ける。⑦⑧は「してもらう」，⑨は「されてしまう」，⑩は「させる」，⑪⑫は「する」（「してしまう」），⑬は「してしまう」の例。

■ ⑭ 〈S be V（過去分詞形）doing (by ~)〉の型の文。

4 Exercises

次の文を指定された語数で英訳しましょう。（　　　　）内で示されている語は必要に応じて，形を変えたうえで用いてください。

① 私は警官が3人の男を追いかけているのを見た。（7語／see）

....

② 彼は女の子が美しい歌を歌っているのを聞いた。（8語）

....

③ 君の名前が呼ばれるのが聞こえなかったかい？（6語）

....

④ 君は目を診察してもらうべきだ。(6 語／ get)

....

⑤ 彼女はこの空港で財布を盗まれた。(8 語／ have)

....

⑥ 目を閉じておきなさい。(4 語)

....

⑦ 私は彼が眠ったままにしておいた。(4 語)

....

⑧ 私はエンジンを 30 分間かけっぱなしにしておいた。(8 語／ keep)

....

⑨ 彼は大声で泣いているのを家族に聞かれた。(8 語／ cry)

....

⑩ 彼女は自分の寝室で 1 人で踊っているのを見られた。(8 語)

....

CHAPTER 5
隠れている疑問文を探せ！

when, where, who, what, why, how のいわゆる 5W1H を使った表現が，少し形を変えて文の中に埋め込まれるいわゆる間接疑問文。この用法を使いこなせれば，婉曲的な疑問表現，配慮にあふれた疑問表現が可能になる。

1 Opening Dialogue ▷▷▷▷▷▷ 大学生こそ夏休みに旅をすべき

★ 下線を引いた文に注意し，表現を覚えよう

Masao: I know you always go somewhere during the summer vacation. Have you got any plans to go someplace this year?

Misaki: Definitely. Where do you think I'm planning to go?

Masao: I wonder. Freshman year, you went to Spain and Portugal, and last year you went to Germany. Somewhere in Europe again this year? 5

Misaki: No, this time it'll be Southeast Asia. I've worked a lot part-time, and I think I've saved enough money, but the only thing I've actually decided is to make Thailand my base—from there I'll just follow my mood at the time.

Masao: That sounds great!

Misaki: But, you know, I've never traveled like that before, and quite honestly, I'm 10 feeling a little anxious about the whole thing. I don't know how much it will all cost, and I might not be able to figure out where I should go next while I'm over there.

Masao: That may be so, but isn't this about the only time in your life when you'll be able to think about making that kind of trip? Once you're out in the real world, 15 you won't be able to just travel around on a whim like that.

Misaki: That's true. This year and next will be my last chances. That's why I've decided to go all out now. How about you? Are you going to do any traveling?

Masao: Yes, but not overseas. I'm planning to borrow my dad's car and make the rounds of all six Tōhoku prefectures. 20

Misaki: That sounds like fun. Will you be going by yourself?

Masao: No, I have a cousin my age who says he wants to go, and it'll be the two of us. I'm glad of that because the driving won't be so boring with someone to talk to.

Misaki: Which prefecture do you think might be the most fun? 25

Masao: I don't know. Each seems to be really nice.

Misaki: I can't wait for the summer vacation! When we get back, we can tell each other all about what kind of trips we had.

Masao: Okay. That'll be fun.

NOTES ———

3 **definitely**「まさに（ある）」／ 11 **anxious**「不安な」／ 12 **figure out**「考えて分かる」／
16 **whim**「思い付き，気まぐれ」／ 25 **prefecture**「県」

 # **2 Understanding More Variations**

次の英文を読み，（　　　）内の和訳を参考に，英単語を並べ替えてみよう。なお，
文頭に置かれる語は大文字で始めてください。

Dialogue A みんなスペイン料理が好き？

A: We're going to have a dinner party for Ms Itō, but I'm not sure what place to have it at. A while ago, I found a nice looking Spanish restaurant near the university, but (1. 先生，スペイン料理好きかな).

B: I don't imagine that'd be a problem. I've never heard of anyone who disliked Spanish food.

A: I guess you're right. I'll make it there, then.

　1. (wonder / likes / I / if / she / food / Spanish)

....

Dialogue B 顧客メモは大事です

A: What's this notebook for, Boss?

B: （2. これはどんなお客さんが来たかを記録するためのものなんだ）.

A: Does everyone who runs a restaurant keep something like this?

B: （3. みんなかどうかはわからないけど）, but I think a lot of them do.

2. (customers / what / it's / keep / had / a record of / kind of / we / to)

....

3. (everyone / don't / if / does / know / I)

....

 3 # Focus on Grammar

文法を理解しよう

★ 間接疑問文

(Q&A)

Q1 Who is he? という疑問文（疑問詞疑問文）を他の文の中に埋め込んで，名詞と同じよう
    に S（主語），C（補語），O（目的語），前置詞の目的語として用いる場合，どのような形
    になるか。

Q2 Where does he live? を間接疑問文にすると，どのような形になるか。

Q3 以下の 2 文のように，前置詞で始まる疑問文を名詞節にする場合，前置詞は移動させる
    必要があるか。

    For what are you working so hard?

    On which street does he live?

Q4 Does he have a car? を間接疑問文にすると，どのような形になるか。

Q5 Is he a doctor or a teacher? を間接疑問文にすると，どのような形になるか。

Q6 間接疑問文が主語の文を，形式主語構文にすることは可能か。

A1 who he is
    ・疑問詞疑問文において，S の前に be 動詞，will, can, should などの助動詞がある場合
     は，これを S の後ろに戻すと名詞節（名詞と同じようにはたらくまとまり）となる。
     このようにして疑問文を名詞節にしたものを「間接疑問文」という。

A2 where he lives
    ・疑問詞疑問文において S の前に does, did, do が出ている場合は，次の基準で名詞節
     （間接疑問文）にする。

    > S の前に does が出ている場合 → does を消去して動詞に -s を加える。
    > S の前に did が出ている場合 → did を消去して動詞を過去形にする。
    > S の前に do が出ている場合 → do を消去する。

・一方で，主語を尋ねる文や主語に対する修飾語を尋ねる文は，主語の前に be 動詞，述語，does, did, do が出ていないので，そのままの形で間接疑問文となる。具体例を挙げる。

> Who invented this tool? ［疑問文］
> ※主語の部分を尋ねている疑問文（who は主語としてはたらいている）

この疑問文を間接疑問にすると，次のようになる。

> → who invented this tool ［間接疑問文］

もう一例見よう。

> Whose bag is the heaviest? ［疑問文］
> ※主語に対する修飾語の部分を尋ねている疑問文（whose は主語 bag に対する修飾語としてはたらいている）

この疑問文を間接疑問にすると，次のようになる。

> → whose bag is the heaviest ［間接疑問文］

A3 ない

For what are you working so hard? を間接疑問文にすると次のようになる。

> → for what you are working so hard ［間接疑問文］

On which street does he live? を間接疑問文にすると次のようになる。

> → on which street he lives ［間接疑問文］

A4 whether [if] he has a car (or not)

・yes-no 疑問文（yes か no かを尋ねる疑問文。「真偽疑問文」とも呼ばれる）を間接疑問文にするための手順は次のようになる。

手順1 疑問詞疑問文を間接疑問文にする場合と同じように，S の前にある be 動詞，助動詞，does, did, do を主語の後ろに戻す，消す，そのうえで動詞の形を変えるなどの作業をする。

手順2 先頭に whether [if] を置く。

手順3 文末に or not を置いてもよい。whether の場合，or not は whether の直後に置くことも可。

※ if 節は O または C としてのみ用いることができる。

・この whether, if は，名詞節を形成する従位接続詞である。

A5 whether he is a doctor or a teacher

・選択疑問文（〈A or B〉の形で選択肢を与えて，相手に選んでもらう疑問文）を間接疑問文にする場合の手順は，yes-no 疑問文を間接疑問文にするための手順に準じる。

A6 可能

① <u>When he left the room</u> is a mystery.

② My question is <u>what color she likes</u>.

③ We don't know <u>what this is</u>.

④ Could you tell me <u>how old John is</u>?

⑤ I want you to explain <u>why you kept silent during the meeting</u>.

⑥ Do you know <u>who painted this picture</u>?

⑦ We talked about <u>which finger is the most useful for humans</u>.

⑧ I don't know <u>with whom I can share my feelings</u>.

⑨ Could you tell me <u>at which station I should change trains</u>?

⑩ <u>Whether she will be successful</u> is far from clear.

⑪ The point is <u>whether he will come or not</u>.

⑫ The problem is <u>whether or not he can finish writing the manuscript by the deadline</u>.

⑬ I wonder <u>if he is able to concentrate well at work</u>.

⑭ I don't know <u>whether it is a dog or a wolf</u>.

⑮ It's unknown <u>where all this information came from</u>.

⑯ It remains to be seen <u>whether my efforts will have any impact in that direction</u>.

解説

■ ①②③④⑤　元が疑問詞疑問文である間接疑問文が用いられた文。間接疑問文（下線部）はそれぞれ S, C, O, O₂（第 4 文型の 2 つ目の O），O としてはたらいている。それぞれの元の疑問文は次の通り。

　　When did he leave the room?

　　What color does she like?

　　What is this?

　　How old is John?

　　Why did you keep silent during the meeting?

■ ⑥⑦　元が疑問詞疑問文である間接疑問文が用いられた文だが，元の疑問詞疑問文が，主語を尋ねるもの（⑥）と，主語に対する修飾語を尋ねるもの（⑦）なので，疑問文がそのままの形で間接疑問文となっている。それぞれの元の疑問文は次の通り。

　　Who painted this picture?　※ who は主語

　　Which finger is the most useful for humans?　※ which は主語 finger を修飾する

　なお⑦の間接疑問文は，前置詞の目的語としてはたらいている。

- ⑧⑨　元が疑問詞疑問文である間接疑問文が用いられた文だが，疑問詞疑問文の先頭が前置詞であるもの。それぞれの元の疑問文は次の通り。

  With whom can I share my feelings?

  At which station should I change trains?

- ⑩⑪⑫⑬　元が yes-no 疑問文である間接疑問文が用いられた文。⑩，⑪，⑫では接続詞として whether が，⑬では if が用いられている。

  ⑩⑪は whether の内部に or not が存在する。⑫では whether の直後に置かれている。

- ⑭　元が選択疑問文である間接疑問文が用いられた文。

- ⑮⑯　真主語が間接疑問文である形式主語構文。

4 Exercises

次の文を指定された語数で英訳しましょう。（　　　　）内で示されている語は必要に応じて，形を変えたうえで用いてください。

① 私たちは彼女がどこ出身なのか分からない。（7 語／ don't）

....

② 誰がこの絵を描いたかは大きな謎だ。（8 語／ big mystery）

....

③ どこに警察署があるかご存じですか？（8 語／ a, station）

....

④ 彼は私にお金を選ぶか名誉を選ぶかを尋ねた。（10 語／ would）

....

⑤ 私の疑問は彼が中国人なのか日本人なのかということだ。（11 語／ a, a）

....

⑥ 私は彼女に彼がどれくらい速く走れるかを告げた。（8 語）

....

⑦ 私たちは彼が金持ちなのかどうかについて語った。(9 語)

  ....

⑧ 誰か，これが誰の曲か知っていますか。(7 語)

  ....

⑨ 私たちはなぜ彼がそんなにも音楽に情熱的なのかについて話した。(10 語／ passionate)

  ....

⑩ 彼がいつ戻ってくるかを私に教えてもらえますか。(8 語)

  ....

CHAPTER 6
関係代名詞をまとめて覚えよう

which, who, that, what などを関係代名詞として用いる表現は，英会話・英作文に必須のものです。より正確で複雑な内容を伝えるために，基本的な用法を押さえておきましょう。

1 Opening Dialogue ▷▷▷▷▷▷ 京都タワーに行くのは最終日に

★ 下線を引いた文に注意し，表現を覚えよう

Masaomi: Kyoto Station! And it only took us a little over two hours from Tokyo!

Mari: A fairly quick trip, wasn't it? Let's head right over to the bus terminal. Mai and Toshihiko wrote that they were already at the museum.

　　　　[*Three minutes later*.]

Masaomi: Here we are. Just look at all the buses! 　　　　　　　　　　　　　　　5

Mari: And they have a huge number of different routes, too.

Masaomi: I don't know which one to take. <u>Where does the one that goes to the Kyoto National Museum leave from?</u>

Mari: I think we can find out on the Museum's homepage. I've got it right here on my smartphone. 　　　　　　　　　　　　　　　　　　　　　　　　　　10

Masaomi: Thanks.

Mari: Here it is. The D2 stop.

Masaomi: D2 is over there. But what's that big tower?

Mari: You don't know? That's Kyoto Tower.

Masaomi: Is it new? 　　　　　　　　　　　　　　　　　　　　　　　　　　　15

Mari: Not at all. They finished it way back in 1964.

Masaomi: It's that old? I never knew anything about it.

Mari: <u>Last year my mom showed me pictures that she had taken from up on the observation deck.</u>

Masaomi: How about if we go there tomorrow? 　　　　　　　　　　　　　　　20

Mari: No, I think we should do that on the last day of the trip.

Masaomi: Why?

Mari: On our last day, we can look down on all the places that we visited and see how they look from above.

Masaomi: That sounds good. It will be fun to see where they all are in relation to 25 one another.

Mari: I think so, too. That will be something to look forward to doing on our last day.

Masaomi: Okay. But now let's get started by getting over to the Museum.

Mari: Right. And here's our bus. All aboard! 30

NOTES ───────

2 **head**「向かう，前進する」／ 16 **way back**「はるか以前」／ 25 **in relation to** ~「~に関係している」

 ## Understanding More Variations

次の英文を読み，（   ）内の和訳を参考に，英単語を並べ替えてみよう。なお，文頭に置かれる語は大文字で始めてください。

Dialogue A ウィリアム征服王とは？

A: It says here "William the Conqueror." Who's that?

B: （1. 彼はイングランドのノルマン朝の最初の王になった人物だよ）. He "conquered" the country in the 11th century. Didn't you learn about him in high school, in World History? It's the one thing that everybody knows about British history.

A: I only studied Japanese History. That was my university entrance exam elective. And even now I *still* know almost nothing about the history of Britain, despite the fact that I'm in the English Department.

B: It's never too late to start. You should at least try to learn some of the fundamentals of European history in general.

1. (the first / who / he / the man / Norman king of England / became / was)

....

●**NOTES**
conquer「征服する」／ **elective**「選択科目」／ **fundamental**「基礎，基本」

Dialogue B 経済学を学ぶにも世界史の知識は大切

A: I realize now that a knowledge of world history is important even in the Economics Department.

B: That's right. I remember being faced, in my freshman year, with a test question that had me at a complete loss: " (2. マルクスがいっしょに『共産党宣言』を書いた人は誰か) "?

A: We should have studied world history more seriously when we were still in high school.

    2. (Marx / is / who / with whom / wrote / *The Communist Manifesto* / the person)

....

●**NOTES**
at a loss「困って，途方に暮れて」

Dialogue C こんな劇場見てみたい

A: What is this photo of?

B: It's of an ancient theater in Türkiye. It's made of stone.

A: I see. (3. この部分が，人々が演じた舞台だね)?

B: Yes. I'd love to go to see a theater like this with my own eyes.

    3. (people / this area / is / stage / which / performed / the / on)

....

3 Focus on Grammar

文法を理解しよう

★関係代名詞

Q&A

Q1 「この家に住んでいる少年」と，a boy <u>who lives in this house</u> では，修飾語と被修飾語の位置関係や，下線部の構造にどのような違いがあるか。

Q2 目的格の関係代名詞は，2 つの品詞の目的語として用いられる。その品詞は何か。

Q3 主格の関係代名詞の具体例と，目的格の関係代名詞の具体例を答えよ。

Q4 所有格の関係代名詞の whose の直後には，ある品詞の語が置かれる。その品詞は何か。

Q5 関係代名詞の that 節または which 節の先行詞が thing である場合，thing + that/ which を 1 語にすると，どのような語になるか。

A1 日本語では名詞を修飾する節（形容詞節）は名詞の前に置かれるのに対し，英語では後ろに置かれる。また，英語では形容詞節をまとめる言葉として関係代名詞が存在するが，日本語には関係代名詞に相当する語は存在しない。

A2 動詞，前置詞

A3 主格の関係代名詞 → who, that, which

目的格の関係代名詞 → whom [who], that, which

・先行詞（関係代名詞節によって修飾される名詞）が人である場合，主格の関係代名詞は who を用いるのが普通（that はあまり用いられない）。人でない場合は that と which のいずれもが用いられるが，that がより好まれる。

・先行詞が人である場合は，目的格の関係代名詞は whom または who が用いられる。whom のほうが正しいが，堅く感じられる場合がある。なお，前置詞の直後には who は用いられない。先行詞が人でない場合の使用基準は主格の場合と同じ。ただし，前置詞の直後には that は用いられないことに注意。

A4 名詞

・whose の訳は，形容詞節を形成しつつ，この名詞に対する修飾語としてはたらく。

A5 what

・what 節は間接疑問文（第 5 章参照）の場合は「何が／を／になど〜ということ」となるが，もう 1 つ「〜こと／もの」と訳す場合もある。この what は，that/which が先行詞 thing を取り込んだ関係代名詞だと考えられる。

例文

① There were some girls around me who were chatting.

② This is a train that [which] goes to the airport.

③ There are few persons whom [who] Mary respects.

④ What is the book that [which] you are going to read tonight?

⑤ The man whom [who] Meg danced with yesterday was Bob.

⑥ What is the subject that [which] you are most interested in?

⑦ Do you know the man with whom Meg went to Kyoto last week?

⑧ What is the purpose for which God created us?

⑨ This is a book my father published last year.

⑩ You may be a person he really needs.

⑪ The hotel we stayed at last year was wonderful.

⑫ I know a person whose father is a legendary baseball player.

⑬ There were some words whose meanings I did not know.

⑭ What he said was true.

⑮ Show me what you have in your pocket.

解説

- ①② 主格の関係代名詞が用いられた文。
- ③④ 目的格の関係代名詞が用いられた文。
- ⑤⑥ ③④と同様に，目的格の関係代名詞が用いられた文だが，前置詞の目的語としてはたらくもの。それぞれ with, in の目的語としてはたらく。
- ⑦⑧ 目的格の関係代名詞（前置詞の目的語としてはたらくもの）が用いられた文だが，前置詞が関係代名詞の前に置かれているもの。この場合，必ず whom か which を用いる。
- ⑨⑩⑪ 目的格の関係代名詞の省略が見られる文。⑨では book の後ろに that [which] が省略されている。⑩では person の後ろに whom [who] が省略されている。⑪では hotel の後ろに that [which] が省略されている。それぞれ動詞 published，動詞 needs，前置詞 at の目的語としてはたらく。
- ⑫⑬ 所有格の関係代名詞 whose が用いられた文。⑫の whose によって修飾されている father は主語。⑬の whose によって修飾されている meanings は know の目的語。このように whose の直後の名詞は，主に主語または目的語としてはたらく。
- ⑭⑮ 関係代名詞 what が用いられた文。⑭では what he said のまとまりが主語としてはたらく。⑮では what you have in your pocket のまとまりが目的語（show の2つ目の目的語）としてはたらく。それぞれの what は「こと」「もの」と訳す。

4 Exercises

次の文を指定された語数で英訳しましょう。（　　　　　）内で示されている語は必要に応じて，形を変えたうえで用いてください。

① この本はスラムに住んでいる男によって書かれた。（12 語）

....

② 私はメグがその教室で話しかけた男の子の名前を知りたい。（16 語／ speak）

....

....

③ 私は見た目が良くて，速く走る車が欲しい。（10 語／ go）

....

④ これは父が若い時に母に送った手紙だ。（15 語）

....

....

⑤ あれはジャックが昨日話していた車だ。（10 語／ talk）

....

⑥ 名前を思い出せない人にどうやって話しかけようか。（10 語／ someone, address）

....

⑦ 昨日ここで起こったことを私に言いなさい。（6 語）

....

⑧ これは地震によって破壊された家の写真だ。（13 語／ destroy）

....

⑨ あなたは彼がその雑誌に書いたものを読みたいですか。（11 語）

....

⑩ 浩二はその声が力強くも繊細でもある歌手だ。（11 語／ powerful）

....

CHAPTER 7
where を「どこ」と訳さないとき

疑問詞としてなじんでいる where, why, when などは，接続詞と副詞の働きをもつ関係副詞として使われる場合があります。関係代名詞との違いも意識しながら，用法を考えてみましょう。

1 *Opening Dialogue* ▷▷▷▷▷▷ 動物病院は水鳥を診てくれるか？

★ 下線を引いた文に注意し，表現を覚えよう

Kohta: Mom, I'm home!

Nobuko: Hi! What's that?

Kohta: A duck.

Nobuko: A duck!?! Why did you bring something like that home?

Kohta: <u>The university has a big pond where a lot of waterbirds live</u>, and today I 5
found this one looking half dead, just lying there all limp along the edge of the
pond.

Nobuko: But what are you planning on doing with it?

Kohta: I want to take it to an animal hospital, but I can't now because I have to get
over to my part-time job right away. 10

Nobuko: Can't you just explain the situation to them and start your shift a little late?

Kohta: No. <u>This is the season when we have the most customers of all.</u> It's the peak
tourist season, and we're really shorthanded.

Nobuko: I see.

Kohta: We're barely able to keep up as it is. I wouldn't want to be late, not even a 15
little. I hate to ask, but could you take it to an animal hospital for me?

Nobuko: Sure, but which one would be good?

Kohta: <u>There was that place where we always used to go when we had Tama.</u> Do
you remember? What was it called?

Nobuko: Sakura Animal Hospital. 20

Kohta: That's right—"Sakura Animal Hospital."

Nobuko: I know they treat dogs and cats, but I wonder if they take other animals, too, like birds.

Kohta: I don't know, but I think they probably do. I remember that one time when I took Tama there I saw that someone had brought in a bird in a big cage.　25

Nobuko: Okay, I'll go right away.

Kohta: Thanks! And I'll get to my job. But I'm worried about this duck's condition. Could you let me know on LINE what they find out?

Nobuko: That wouldn't be any problem, but can you be checking LINE while you're at work?　30

Kohta: Not when I'm working, of course, but I can check it during my break.

NOTES

3 **duck**「カモ，アヒルなど水鳥の総称」／ 6 **limp**「元気のない，弱々しい」／ 9 **get over to ~**「～に行く」／ 15 **keep up as it is**「今のままでやっていく」

 2　Understanding More Variations

次の英文を読み，（　　　）内の和訳を参考に，英単語を並べ替えてみよう。なお，文頭に置かれる語は大文字で始めてください。

Dialogue A　アメフトはなぜ人気？

A:（1. アメリカンフットボールがアメリカで断トツ一番人気のスポーツである理由が全くわからないよ）.

B: You can't understand that because you don't know the rules of football. If you did, you'd realize how exciting the sport really is.

A: Maybe I'll try to learn the rules, then.

1.（ can't / the reason / popular / I / why / in / football / is / the most / understand / sport / the U.S. / by far ）

....

....

Dialogue B　みんな，あなたのことお見通しです

A: （2. そこが君が間違っている箇所だよ）. Don't you realize what a mistake you made then?

B: I don't understand.

A: You should never try to impress people by pretending to be someone you aren't. They'll almost always see right through you.

2. (it / the / you / got / point / where / wrong / that's)

⋯⋯⋯⋯⋯⋯⋯⋯⋯⋯⋯⋯⋯⋯⋯⋯⋯⋯⋯⋯⋯⋯⋯⋯⋯⋯⋯⋯⋯⋯⋯⋯

● **NOTES**

see through ~「~（の本性・たくらみなど）を見通す，見透かす」

Dialogue C　おすすめは『深夜特急』

A: I'm looking for some good travel writing to read over the holidays. Can you recommend anything?

B: I think you should try Sawaki Kōtarō's *Shin'yatokkyū.*

A: What's it about?

B: （3. インドのデリーからロンドンまで乗合バスで行く様子が描かれているんだ）. It still has a lot of avid fans.

3. (he / the way / London / regular passenger bus / that / it's / traveled / Delhi in India / to / from / by / about)

⋯⋯⋯⋯⋯⋯⋯⋯⋯⋯⋯⋯⋯⋯⋯⋯⋯⋯⋯⋯⋯⋯⋯⋯⋯⋯⋯⋯⋯⋯⋯⋯

⋯⋯⋯⋯⋯⋯⋯⋯⋯⋯⋯⋯⋯⋯⋯⋯⋯⋯⋯⋯⋯⋯⋯⋯⋯⋯⋯⋯⋯⋯⋯⋯

● **NOTES**
avid「熱心な，熱烈な」

3 *Focus on Grammar*

文法を理解しよう

★ 関係副詞

Q&A

Q1 形容詞節（名詞を修飾する節）の where 節は，どのような名詞を修飾するか。

Q2 形容詞節の when 節は，どのような名詞を修飾するか。

Q3 形容詞節の why 節は，どの名詞を修飾するか。

Q4 「S が V する方法／様子」に対する英訳として〈way + how 節〉は適切か。

Q5 形容詞節を形成する関係副詞は省略することが可能か。

Q6 関係副詞の where 節，when 節，why 節，how 節が名詞節として機能する場合，これらはどのような訳になるか。

A1 場所に関する名詞。point（箇所），part（部分），situation（状況），circumstances（環境）など，比喩的な意味での "場" を表す語をも修飾する。

A2 時に関する名詞

A3 reason

A4 適切ではない。
・「S が V する方法／様子」は〈way + that 節〉で表現する。

A5 可能
・特に when（先行詞が具体的な年月日，時間ではない場合），why，that が頻繁に省略される。where も先行詞が place である場合は省略が可能。

A6 「…場所」「…時」「…理由」「…方法［様子］」

例文

① This is the coffee shop where I met John.

② This is the part where I cried.

③ Last year was the year when I first went abroad.

④ I was born in 1939, when World War II began.

⑤ Do you know the reason why Jack quit his part-time job?

⑥ This is the way that he opened the box.

⑦ Do you remember the day you first saw me?

⑧ There is no reason I should be blamed.

⑨ The way he spoke was very soft and thoughtful.

⑩ This is the place I feel most comfortable.

⑪ Where I was born was a small town.

⑫ This is a picture of when I was young.

⑬ He is always kind to everybody. That is why we respect him.

⑭ How she answered was impressive.

解説

- ①② 形容詞節の where 節が用いられている文。②の先行詞（修飾される名詞）は物理的な意味での場所ではなく，「部分」「箇所」という意味。

- ③④ 形容詞節の when 節が用いられている文。

- ⑤ 形容詞節の why 節が用いられている文。

- ⑥ 形容詞節の that 節が用いられている文。

- ⑦⑧⑨⑩ 関係副詞の省略が見られる文。day の後ろに when, reason の後ろに why, way の後ろに that, place の後ろに where が省略されている。

- ⑪⑫⑬⑭ 関係副詞の where 節，when 節，why 節，how 節が，名詞節として用いられている文。それぞれ S, 前置詞の目的語, C, S としてはたらいている。

4 Exercises

次の文を指定された語数で英訳しましょう。（　　　　）内で示されている語は必要に応じて，形を変えたうえで用いてください。

① 私たちはテニスができる公園を探している。（11 語／ look）

....

② 彼が生きていた状況は過酷なものだった。（7 語／ severe）

....

③ 君が僕に会った夜のことを覚えているか？（9 語）

....

④ 夫がそんなにも電車が好きな理由が私には理解できなかった。(12 語／ much)

　　………………………………………………………………………………………

⑤ 私は彼の歌い方が好きではない。(7 語)

　　………………………………………………………………………………………

⑥ 彼はいつもみんなに親切だ。それが，私たちが彼のことを好きな理由だ［そういう訳で，私たちは彼のことを好きだ］。(6 語)※下線部のみを訳す

　　………………………………………………………………………………………

⑦ 彼女はその箱を 3 回蹴った。それが，彼女が箱を開けた方法だ［そういうふうにして彼女は箱を開けた］。(7 語)※下線部のみを訳す

　　………………………………………………………………………………………

⑧ 私たちは彼の馬たちが走る様子に魅了された。(9 語／ fascinated, way)

　　………………………………………………………………………………………

⑨ 私は自分が立っているところからそのタワーが見えない。(10 語)

　　………………………………………………………………………………………

⑩ 4 月は日本で学校が始まる時だ。(7 語)

　　………………………………………………………………………………………

CHAPTER 8
決意や条件を述べるとき使える表現とは？

as far as, even if, など, いわゆる従位接続詞を使った表現は, 「時」「条件」「譲歩」「理由」「目的」などを表す際に便利です。when, while, before, after, because など, 初歩的な従位接続詞より一歩上のレベルのものを用いた副詞節を使いこなせるようになりましょう。

1 Opening Dialogue ▷▷▷▷▷▷▷ 芸術の道で生きていく覚悟

★ 下線を引いた文に注意し, 表現を覚えよう

Kazuo: There are only five of us part-timers where I work, and, surprisingly, three are fine arts or music majors. Aren't you a violin major?

Riho: That's right. And I think you're doing traditional Japanese-style painting.

Kazuo: No. Actually, I major in oil painting. Are you planning on making a living with the violin? 5

Riho: I was planning to do that at first, which is why I decided to go to a school of music, but I've given up on the idea.

Kazuo: Why? You're studying at a famous school of music, but you don't plan to be a professional? You're not going to do concerts or put out CDs?

Riho: I wouldn't ever be able to make it that far. Only a very few graduates 10 actually manage to succeed on their own as professional musicians. Some of my classmates are unbelievably talented, and as I've watched them, I've come to realize the sad fact that I don't really have what it takes.

Kazuo: How about just joining an orchestra, then?

Riho: That's awfully hard, too. It's a terribly competitive field. 15

Kazuo: So, in the future, you're planning on doing something completely unrelated to music?

Riho: Probably. Unfortunately, the chances of my doing that are high. <u>I'll keep playing the violin as long as I live, though.</u> How about you? Are you going to try to live as a painter? 20

Kazuo: I'll be happy if I can. I'd like to be able to live on the sales of my paintings.

Riho: But, in the art world, isn't it hard to turn your name into a sellable "brand"?

Kazuo: It's very, very hard. I know that. It would be like a miracle to be able to do it. But I still want to try.

Riho: What do you need to do to get a good start?

Kazuo: First of all, I'll have to have won a prize at a major competition by the time that I graduate.

Riho: I don't think it's out of the realm of possibilities for you to win a prize like that. Everybody knows how serious you are about your art, and you always get right back to your painting just as soon as you get home after your part-time job.

Kazuo: Well, I do have a pretty strict work ethic, and unless I really devote myself to constant practice, I don't think I'll ever be able to create any truly meaningful paintings.

Riho: The path of an artist is never an easy one. It's more than just having skills—it involves your whole way of life, too, doesn't it?

NOTES ─────────

4 **major in** ~「～を専攻する」／ 10 **make it**「成功する，やり遂げる」／ 13 **what it takes**「必要な資質・能力」／ 28 **realm**「範囲, 領域」／ 31 **devote**「打ち込む, 捧げる」

2 *Understanding More Variations*

次の英文を読み，（　　）内の和訳を参考に，英単語を並べ替えてみよう。なお，文頭に置かれる語は大文字で始めてください。

Dialogue A 復活を遂げる観光業界

A: I seem to see a lot more foreign tourists around the city lately.

B: That's right. The tourism industry has gradually been recovering following the dark days of the COVID-19 pandemic.

A: When in the past did Japan have the most visitors from abroad?

B: (1. 私の知る限り，それは 2019 年で，その時 3 千万人を優に超えていました).

　1. (30 million / it / in 2019, / was / there were / as far as / well over / I know, / when)

....

Dialogue B　猛暑に欠かせないものとは

A: It's really been too hot this summer, hasn't it.

B: I've been sweltering! I hope I don't get heat stroke!

A: I keep an extra supply of bottled water at home and always carry plenty of water with me (2. 確実に十分な水分補給ができるように).

　　2. (that / well hydrated / to / make sure / so / I / can / stay)

⋯⋯⋯⋯⋯⋯⋯⋯⋯⋯⋯⋯⋯⋯⋯⋯⋯⋯⋯⋯⋯⋯⋯⋯⋯⋯⋯⋯⋯⋯⋯⋯⋯⋯⋯

●NOTES

swelter「暑さにうだる，暑さでぐったりする」／ **heat stroke**「熱中症」／ **hydrated**「水分が与えられた」

Dialogue C　就職活動について考え始めるとき

A: You seem to be looking a little glum lately. What's the matter?

B: (2. 大学3年になったからには，就職活動について真剣に考えなければならないんだ), and I'm not at all confident that I'll be able to handle it very well.

A: Most people feel that way. I'm sure that once you get started, you'll find that job hunting is not as hard as you thought it would be.

　　3. (think seriously / now / about / in my junior year, / job hunting / I / to / have / I'm / that)

⋯⋯⋯⋯⋯⋯⋯⋯⋯⋯⋯⋯⋯⋯⋯⋯⋯⋯⋯⋯⋯⋯⋯⋯⋯⋯⋯⋯⋯⋯⋯⋯⋯⋯⋯

●NOTES

glum「陰気な，ふさぎ込んだ」／ **handle**「うまく扱う」

 # Focus on Grammar

文法を理解しよう

★副詞節を形成するいろいろな従位接続詞

(Q&A)

Q1　「～するために」の意味は to V で表すことができるが，「Xが～するために」の意味を節（内側に SV が存在するまとまり）で表現する場合，どのような形になるか。

Q2 「〜までに」を表す前置詞は by だが，「X が〜するまでに」はどのような形で表すか。

Q3 as [so] long as と as [so] far as はいずれも「〜する限り」と訳されるが，どのように意味が異なるか。

Q4 事実上の従位接続詞として用いられる even if と even though はどのように意味が異なるか。

Q5 副詞節を形成する従位接続詞（あるいは事実上の従位接続詞だと考えられるもの）として，他に unless, once, as soon as, the moment, in case, now that などが挙げられるが，それぞれどのような意味をもつか。

A1 so that SV または in order that SV

・so that の 2 語，in order that の 3 語でまとめて 1 つの従位接続詞だと考えることができる。so that のほうが多く用いられ，in order that はやや堅く感じられる表現である。

A2 by the time (that) SV

・by the time もやはり，3 語で事実上の従位接続詞だと考えることができる。

A3 as [so] long as は「時間」「条件」を表す。as [so] far as は「空間［距離］」「範囲」を表す。

・これらも同様に，ひとまとまりの従位接続詞だといえる。

A4 even if は「たとえ〜ではあっても」。even though は「〜だが」。even though は though を強めた形。これも「たとえ〜ではあっても」と訳される場合はあるが，even if があくまで仮定について述べるのに対し，even though は「（実際）〜だが」のように〈事実〉について述べていることに注意。

A5 unless（〜しない限り），once（いったん〜すると），as soon as（〜するとすぐに），the moment（〜するとすぐに），in case（〜した場合は，〜した場合に備えて），now that（今やもう〜なので）。

例文

① He is working hard so that his family can live comfortably.

② I must finish this job by the time he returns here.

③ I'll listen to his songs as long as I live.

④ You can stay here as long as you don't cause trouble.

⑤ There was water as far as my eyes could see.

⑥ As far as I know, my father has never been abroad.

⑦ Now that you are 20, I'll treat you as an adult.

⑧ He never speaks unless he has something profound to say.

⑨ Once you form a bad habit, it's incredibly difficult to break it.

⑩ As soon as he arrived at the station, he was surrounded by a massive crowd.

⑪ The moment I opened the door, my dog came running toward me.

⑫ In case you need my help, don't hesitant to contact me.

⑬ I just want to be there in case something special happens.

⑭ Even if I were a millionaire, I wouldn't buy a yacht.

⑮ Even though the weather was bad, we had a great holiday.

解説

■ ①　副詞節を形成する従位接続詞の so that が用いられた文。

■ ②　副詞節を形成する従位接続詞の by the time が用いられた文。

■ ③ ④　副詞節を形成する従位接続詞の as long as が用いられた文。③は「時間」，④は「条件」を表す。

■ ⑤ ⑥　副詞節を形成する従位接続詞の as far as が用いられた文。⑤は「空間［距離］」，⑥は「範囲」を表す。

■ ⑦　副詞節を形成する従位接続詞の now that が用いられた文。that は省略されることもある。この場合は名詞，副詞の now との区別がつきにくくなることに注意。

■ ⑧　副詞節を形成する従位接続詞の unless が用いられた文。

■ ⑨　副詞節を形成する従位接続詞の once が用いられた文。once は副詞（かつて，一度，いったん）としても用いられるので，判別が必要になることに注意。

■ ⑩　副詞節を形成する従位接続詞の as soon as が用いられた文。

■ ⑪　副詞節を形成する従位接続詞の the moment が用いられた文。moment は名詞でもあるので，判別が必要になる。

■ ⑫ ⑬　副詞節を形成する従位接続詞の in case が用いられた文。⑫は「～した場合は」の意味。「もし私の助けが必要になったら」などと訳してもよい。後半（don't 以下）は命令文。⑬は「～した場合に備えて」の意味。

■ ⑭ ⑮　副詞節を形成する従位接続詞の even if, even though が用いられた文。

4 Exercises

次の文を指定された語数で英訳しましょう。(　　　　) 内で示されている語は必要に応じて，形を変えたうえで用いてください。

① 君が毎日練習できるように，私は君をサポートします。(11 語／ can)

....

② たとえ昇給があっても，私は仕事をやめるつもりだ。(14 語／ get, pay raise)
　　※ job で文を終える

....

③ そのニュースを聞くとすぐに，彼は病院に急行した。(12 語／ rush)

....

④ 私の知る限り，これが最新版だ。(10 語)

....

⑤ 11 時までに戻ってくると約束するのであれば，外出してよい。(15 語／ can, be)
　　※ o'clock で文を終える

....

⑥ その駅にたどり着くまでに私は完全に疲れ果てていた。(11 語)
　　※ exhausted で文を終える

....

⑦ 道に迷うといけないからこの地図を持っていきなさい。(8 語／ get)
　　※ lost で文を終える

....

⑧ 今や君は大人になったのだから，子供のようにふるまうのはやめるべきだ。
　　　　　　　　　　　　　　　　　　　　　　　　　　(13 語／ adult, behave)

....

⑨ 私のカメラは，何か特別なことが起こらない限り，私のポケットから出てこない。（12 語）

....

⑩ 私は一度始めたら，少なくても 3 時間くらい働き続ける。（12 語／ get, work, about）

....

CHAPTER 9
no matter の用法を極めよう！

近年，Black Lives Matter という表現で話題と論議を呼んだ動詞 matter だが，この単語は，名詞としての用法にも重要なものが多い。否定の no とともに使われる no matter ~ という表現に焦点を当ててみよう。

1 *Opening Dialogue* ▷▷▷▷▷▷ 学園祭には大物ゲストが必要だ

★下線を引いた文に注意し，表現を覚えよう

Yoshiki: What do you think we should have as the main event in this year's school festival? We ought to try to come up with a few ideas to present at tomorrow's Planning Committee meeting.

Rino: Last year we had some *manzai* comedians, but they didn't go over well at all.

Yoshiki: And they weren't even very famous to begin with. The year before that we 5 invited a "pop idol," but she fell ill just before and couldn't come.

Rino: That was a disaster. There was no main event.

Yoshiki: Two failures in a row. We have to get something good this time. You must have a few ideas.

Rino: I think we need some sort of "superstar." How about a lecture by Takamura 10 Ken? A lot of people would come to see *him*.

Yoshiki: No way would he accept. I don't know what he'd say if it were Meijitsu University, his alma mater, but an actor as internationally famous as he would never come to the festival of a school he had no connection to, like ours. Besides, we wouldn't have enough of a budget to get him anyway. 15

Rino: How about if we persuaded the school president to ask him. He might come if he got a direct offer from the president.

Yoshiki: Still no way! No matter who invited him, it would be impossible for *us* to get that kind of "superstar."

Rino: No way, huh? 20

Yoshiki: Hey! Look! A mouse! Next to that cardboard!

Rino: Eek! Get rid of it!

Yoshiki: What should I do? Try to catch it? There—it ran off, under the door.

Rino: I hate mice! They're really scary!

Yoshiki: How can you be scared of something like a mouse?   25

Rino: Anyway, this room's such a dirty mess. That's why it attracts mice.

Yoshiki: We had a mouse in here one time last year, too. Remember? <u>And no matter when we come here, this room is always a dirty mess.</u>

Rino: We need to do something about that. Let's stop our talking for a while and do some cleaning.   30

NOTES ───────

2 **come up with**「思い付く」／ 4 **go over well**「成功を収める，気に入られる」／ 7 **disaster**「大失敗，大惨事」／ 13 **alma mater**「母校（ラテン語より）」

 ## **2** **Understanding More Variations**

次の英文を読み，（　　　）内の和訳を参考に，英単語を並べ替えてみよう。なお，文頭に置かれる語は大文字で始めてください。

Dialogue A　日本の水道水は奇跡の存在

A: I love traveling abroad, but in a lot of places, the tap water is undrinkable, which can be a problem.

B: （1. 日本国内なら，どこに行っても水道水が飲めるもんね）．

A: It certainly is, and after all my overseas experiences, that seems to me to be almost miraculous.

1. (Japan / is / water in / matter / you / drinkable / no / in the country / go / tap / where)

....

● **NOTES**

tap water「水道水」

Dialogue B　金色堂を守りたい

A: Last week, I went to Iwate and saw the Konjikidō Golden Hall on the grounds of Chūson-ji Temple.

B: The Hall itself is completely sheltered by a concrete building, isn't it?

A: That's right. (2. どんな思い切った手段がとられる必要があっても), people are determined to do what is necessary to protect our National Treasures.

2. (be / measures / need / no matter / drastic / might / taken / to / what)

....

● **NOTES**
shelter「保護する」

 Dialogue C　ドイツ語を学ぶ理由

37

A: After graduation, I hope to go to Germany to study music theory.

B: So that's why you're always studying German?

A: It is. I'm considering Austria, too, as another possible country for my music theory studies, but (3. どっちの国を選ぶのであれ, やっぱりドイツ語の知識が必要になるからね).

B: I guess so. German is, after all, also Austria's official language.

3. (need / no matter / I / choose, / will / which / still / to / German / know / I)

....

 3 Focus on Grammar
　　　文法を理解しよう
　　　★副詞節を形成する従位接続詞 no matter ~

(Q&A)

Q1　no matter when は「いつ〜しようとも」, no matter where は「どこで〜しようとも」という意味だが, no matter how はどのような意味か。

Q2　以下の2つでは, no matter who の和訳がどう異なるか。
　　　No matter who says so, I won't do it.
　　　No matter who(m) you meet, you need to treat everyone with the utmost respect.

Q3　no matter what と no matter which は, S, C, O, 前置詞の目的語に加えて, もう1つ別の要素としてはたらく。それは何か。

Q4　no matter ~ 節の述語部分にある助動詞が置かれた場合は, それを訳さない。その助動詞とは何か。

A1 「どのように～しようとも」「どれくらい～しようとも」の２つの意味がある。

・後者の場合，no matter how の直後に形容詞か副詞が存在する。

A2 ①→「誰が（～とも）」。②→「誰に（～とも）」。

・no matter who は，疑問詞の who と同様に S，C，O，前置詞の目的語のいずれかとしてはたらく。はたらきがどれかによって，添える言葉が「が」「を」「だ」「と」など，違いが生じる。①は S なので「が」を添える。②は meet の O なので「に」を添える。

A3 名詞に対する修飾語

・no matter what が名詞に対する修飾語として用いられている場合は「何の［どんな］…が［を，にぉど］～とも」と訳し，no matter which の場合は「どちらの…が［を，にぉど］～とも」と訳す。

・疑問詞の what, which が，S，C，O，前置詞の目的語のみならず，名詞に対する修飾語としてはたらくように（［what の例］What color do you like?［which の例］Which team won?），no matter what と no matter which も，名詞に対する修飾語としてのはたらきをもつ。

A4 may, might

例文

① No matter where you work, you should always try to do your very best.

② I am ready to give you my support no matter when you may need it.

③ No matter how I tried, I couldn't open the window.

④ No one will want to marry him no matter how rich he is.

⑤ No matter how fast you run, you won't be able to catch the train.

⑥ No matter who said so, I don't believe it.

⑦ No matter who you are, you still need to pay the fee.

⑧ No matter who(m) you meet in life, you can always learn something from them.

⑨ No matter what comes next, just be confident and have faith in yourself.

⑩ He has a right to speak on the issue no matter what his opinions might be.

⑪ Don't trust him, no matter what he says.

⑫ No matter what language I've studied, I've always been weak in vocabulary.

⑬ No matter which road you take, you'll be able to get there in about 20 minutes.

- ① no matter where が用いられた文。

- ② no matter when が用いられた文。副詞節である no matter when 節が文の後半にある。no matter when 節内の述語部分に may が存在するが，これは訳さない。

- ③④⑤ no matter how が用いられた文。③の no matter how は「どのように～しようとも」の例。④⑤は「どれくらい～しようとも」の例。④は no matter how の直後に形容詞 rich があり，⑤は直後に副詞 fast がある。④は副詞節が文の後半にある形。

- ⑥⑦⑧ no matter who が用いられた文。no matter who はそれぞれ S，C，O としてはたらいている。それぞれ「誰が～とも」「S が誰であろうとも」「S が誰に～とも」と訳す。

- ⑨⑩⑪⑫ no matter what が用いられた文。no matter what はそれぞれ S，C，O，名詞に対する修飾語としてはたらいている。⑨⑩⑪はそれぞれ「何が～とも」「S が何であろうとも」「S が何を～とも」。⑫の no matter what + language は「どんな言語を～とも」と訳す。「を」が現れるのは，language が have studied の O であるため。
⑩は no matter what 節が文の後半にある。また，この文では no matter what 節内の述語部分に might が存在するが，これは訳さない。

- ⑬ no matter which が用いられた文。no matter which は名詞に対する修飾語としてはたらいている。no matter which + road は「どちらの道路を～とも」と訳す。「を」が現れるのは road が take の O であるため。

4 Exercises

次の文を指定された語数で英訳しましょう。英文はすべて no で始め，（　　　　）内で示されている語は必要に応じて，形を変えたうえで用いてください。

① どこに行っても，普段インターネットは使える。(11 語／ you)

....

② いつ来ても，私たちはあなたを歓迎します。(9 語)

....

③ どんなに忙しくても，私は読書のための時間を見つけることはできますよ。(12 語／ for)

....

④ 誰がここに来ても，私はドアを開けるつもりはない。（10語）

⑤ 誰と働こうとも，あなたは成功する。（9語）

⑥ 何を書くのであれ，綴りのチェックをしなければならない。（10語）

⑦ どちらの大学を選ぶのであれ，あなたは満足するでしょう。（11語／probably）

⑧ 何について語るのであれ，彼は難しい言葉を使わないようにした。
（13語／talk, difficult, word）

⑨ どんな職業を選ぶのであれ，効果的にコミュニケーションをする能力は，すべての雇用者によって高く評価される。（19語／occupation, a person, the ability, value, all）

⑩ どのように彼女を慰めようとしても無駄だった。（12語／I, console, it, help）

CHAPTER 10
「たまたま〜する」と英語で言うには？

> 「〜するようになる」「わざわざ〜する」というようなことを英語で表現したくなったことがあるでしょう。この章では，happen to 〜，come to 〜，be supposed to 〜 など，助動詞と似ている機能をもつ便利な表現を取り上げます。

1 Opening Dialogue ▷▷▷▷▷▷ ジャズピアノ，始めました

★ 下線を引いた文に注意し，表現を覚えよう

Yukari: Yesterday, when I went to the Pegasus Music instrument shop in front of the station, Mari happened to be there.

Masahiko: Pegasus Music? I didn't know you played an instrument.

Yukari: You couldn't really say that I actually "play." I had never taken lessons on any instrument before. But lately I've been learning and listening to jazz piano. 5 I've come to listen to it every day.

Masahiko: Jazz piano—that's nice. I love it, too. I usually listen to it when I'm studying.

Yukari: But I can't be satisfied anymore just listening. Six months ago I started taking lessons. 10

Masahiko: Really! But isn't it a little late in life for you to be just starting?

Yukari: It's true that people do tend to start learning any instrument, not just the piano, at quite an early age.

Masahiko: But it would be great to be able to play one. Didn't somebody once say "If you want to enjoy life, take up, just for pleasure, one foreign language and 15 one musical instrument"?

Yukari: That's interesting advice. I can't seem to enjoy any foreign language, but I feel like I'm getting hooked on the piano.

Masahiko: Are you planning on giving a recital someday?

Yukari: No, nothing so ambitious as that! But I have about ten or so jazz-piano 20 songs that I'm especially fond of, and I'm determined to learn to play them well.

Masahiko: How did you find a teacher?

Yukari: <u>A cousin of mine just happened to have among her friends a young woman who teaches piano.</u> The woman seemed really nice when we were first introduced, and I decided to take lessons from her. We get along well and ₂₅ sometimes even go out places together.

Masahiko: Great—just as if you were friends!

Yukari: That's actually what it feels like. We're fairly close in age and share some of the same interests. <u>In fact, we're scheduled to go together to a jazz recital in Yokohama next week.</u> It's a dinner show. ₃₀

Masahiko: That sounds nice!

Yukari: Sometime maybe I'll invite you out for an evening like that.

Masahiko: Thanks! I'll definitely be looking forward to *that*!

NOTES ————

18 **get hooked on** ~「~に夢中になる，～にはまる」／ 25 **get along well**「仲良くやっていく」／ 26 **go out places**「遊びまわる」

 ## **Understanding More Variations**

次の英文を読み，（　　　）内の和訳を参考に，英単語を並べ替えてみよう。なお，文頭に置かれる語は大文字で始めてください。

Dialogue A　佐藤錦への情熱

A: Hi! I didn't see you in class yesterday. Where've you been?

B: I just got back from Yamagata. I went there to buy "Sato Nishiki" cherries.

A: （1. なんで，わざわざ山形まで行く必要があるの）？ You can get them at most local supermarkets around here.

B: I wanted to pick them myself when they were at their very freshest—and to taste a few, too, while I was doing the picking. It's fun. You should try it sometime.

1. (to / why / to / Yamagata / all the way / go / bother)

....

Dialogue B　なぜ再生可能エネルギーか？

A: （2. 日本は再生可能エネルギーの使用を広げることに熱心のようだね）.

B: You mean sources of energy like solar, wind, and geothermal?

A: Exactly. And that eagerness is only natural since Japan's rate of energy self-sufficiency is so very low.

2. (seems / Japan / be / to / renewable energy / expand / of / eager / its use / to)

....

● NOTES
geothermal 「地熱の」 ／ **rate** 「率，割合」

Dialogue C 大和級の戦艦をもっと作る計画があった

41

A: Did you know there was another battleship that was the same size as the Yamato?

B: I did. Battleship Musashi, right? I read Yoshimura Akira's book about it. (3. 実際のところ，同じサイズの戦艦は，本来は全部で4隻くらい建造することになっていたんだよね).

A: Really!?!

B: It's true. But they only managed to build two, the Yamato and the Musashi, and both of those were sunk by the U.S. Navy.

3. (size / be / supposed / four or so / that / of / same / were / to / built / ships / actually,)

....

3 Focus on Grammar

文法を理解しよう

★助動詞相当表現（動詞＋to，be 動詞＋形容詞／過去分詞形の動詞＋to）

Q&A

Q1 I decided to be there.（私はそこにいようと決めた）と I happened to be there.（私はたまたまそこにいた）では，文の構造がどのように異なるか。

Q2 〈自動詞＋to〉以外で，to を含み，助動詞に相当する表現として，〈be 動詞＋X＋to〉の型を挙げることができるが，X の部分にはどのような品詞の語が置かれるか。

Q3 A2 の具体例にはどのようなものがあるか。

Q4 be about to という表現はどのような意味か。

A1 前者は次のように分析できる。

```
I decided │to be there│.
S   V        O
```

後者は次のように分析できる。

```
I    happened to    be      there.
S  助動詞に相当する表現  V   修飾語 (be を修飾)
```

・happen to（たまたま〜する）と同じグループに入れて考えられるものとして，次のようなものが挙げられる。

seem to（〜するようだ），appear to（〜するようだ），come to（〜するようになる），get to（〜するようになる），learn to（〜するようになる），tend to（〜する傾向がある），bother to（わざわざ〜する）など

A2 形容詞，動詞（主に過去分詞形）。

A3 〈be 動詞＋形容詞＋ to〉の具体例としては，以下のようなものが挙げられる。

be afraid to（〜するのを恐れる，こわくて〜できない），be apt to（〜しがちである），be certain to（きっと〜する），be due to（〜する予定である，〜ことになっている），be eager to（しきりに〜したがる），be free to（自由に〜してもいい），be happy to（喜んで〜する），be likely to（〜しそうである），be unlikely to（〜しそうにない），be ready to（〜する準備ができている），be sure to（きっと〜する），be unable to（〜することができない）

〈be 動詞＋動詞（過去分詞形）＋ to〉の具体例として，次のようなものが挙げられる。

be bound to（〜する義務がある，きっと〜する），be determined to（〜する決心である），be inclined to（〜したい気がする，〜する傾向がある），be meant to（〜することになっている，〜するためのものである），be scheduled to（〜する予定である），be supposed to（〜することになっている）

※〈be 動詞＋動詞（ing 形）＋ to〉の例として，be going to（〜する予定［つもり］だ，〜しそうだ）が挙げられる。

A4 まさに〜しようとする，するところである

例文

① He appears to own a large house.

② He tends to complain about everything.

③ His name came to be known by many people.

④ My son will learn to read and write soon.

⑤ He is sure to win the game.

⑥ You are free to use this car.

⑦ I'll be happy to help you.

⑧ She is eager to meet my son.

⑨ She is likely to accept your request.

⑩ You are bound to succeed in two or three years.

⑪ He is determined to leave this town next month.

⑫ This building is supposed to be used as an office building.

⑬ He is scheduled to stay here for three days.

⑭ When she called me, I was about to leave the office.

解説

■ ①②③④ 〈自動詞 + to〉が含まれる文。①の appear は seem と同義。④の learn to は同じ「〜するようになる」という意味でも，come to や get to とは異なり，「自ら学んで〜する［できる］ようになる」というニュアンスがある。

■ ⑤⑥⑦⑧⑨ 〈be 動詞 + 形容詞 + to〉が含まれる文。

■ ⑩⑪⑫⑬ 〈be 動詞 + 動詞（過去分詞形）+ to〉が含まれる文。

■ ⑭ be about to が含まれる文。

 Exercises

次の文を指定された語数で英訳しましょう。（　　　　　）内で示されている語は必要に応じて，形を変えたうえで用いてください。

① あなた方はどのようにしてお互いを知ったのですか？（8 語／ come）

....

② 彼はこの部屋の中で眠っているようだ。(8 語／ seem)

....

③ 彼らはたまたま同じビルに住んでいた。(8 語)

....

④ 君はどんな分野でも成功しそうだよ。(8 語／ field)

....

⑤ 彼女はきっとあなたを強く支えてくれる。(7 語／ strongly)

....

⑥ うちの息子たちがしきりにあなたに会いたがっているのです。(7 語／ eager)

....

⑦ この列車はまさに駅を出るところだ。(8 語／ leave)

....

⑧ 紙のお金はいつ受け入れられるようになったのか？ (8 語／ money, accept)

....

⑨ 彼はこの本を数回読んだことあるようだ。(9 語／ seem, several)

....

⑩ ほとんどの日本人のドライバーは黄信号で止まらない傾向がある。(10 語)

....

CHAPTER 11

後悔を表す should have, could have の使い方

日本語，英語にかかわらず，日常生活で使う頻度が高い「〜すればよかった」「〜のはずはない」「〜だったに違いない」「きっと〜だったのだろう」というような表現。should, could, must, might などの助動詞と組み合わせてできる用法を考えてみよう。

1 Opening Monologue ▷▷▷▷▷▷▷ 接客業は学びの場

★ 下線を引いた文に注意し，表現を覚えよう

I've been waiting tables part-time for a year now, and working in the service industry has really been an education.

When I have to deal with an arrogant customer, I always feel that I would never want to take an attitude like that myself. When a customer reacts forgivingly to a mistake I've made, I feel I want to learn to behave that way, too. And whenever I 5 happen to thank someone and am thanked back, it makes me want to react in the same way when I'm being served by someone myself. The service industry is truly a place for learning. Now that I only have half a year left before graduating from the university, I can't help feeling that <u>I should have started doing this kind of part-time work a little sooner.</u> 10

It was awfully crowded in the restaurant today. <u>There must have been some big event at the nearby stadium.</u> It's always crowded when the stadium holds an event, but I've never before had to deal with a rush like today's. Still, my experience so far has been that after work on what has been a very busy day, I seem to feel a special sense of fulfillment. Tonight, before going home, I went out with some of my fellow 15 part-timers to a family-style restaurant and enjoyed a meal with them. It was a busy but very nice day.

In the little time I have left before graduation, I want to make the most of my part-time work—to try to learn as much as possible while, at the same time, giving customers an enjoyable experience. 20

NOTES ―――――

3 **arrogant**「傲慢な，横柄な」 ／ 4 **forgivingly**「寛大に」

2 Understanding More Variations

次の英文を読み，（　　）内の和訳を参考に，英単語を並べ替えてみよう。なお，文頭に置かれる語は大文字で始めてください。

Dialogue A　ヒナがいなくなってしまった！

A: Look! All the newborn chicks that were in this swallow's nest yesterday are gone. That's a shame. There are a lot of crows around here, and（1. そのうちの一羽が巣を襲ったのかもしれないな）.

B: Or a snake might have done it.

A: Do snakes attack bird nests?

B: They certainly do. You can see video clips of that on the net.

　　1. (of / I / one / guess / have / them / the nest / might / attacked)

....

　●NOTES
chicks「ヒナ」

Dialogue B　芥川賞と直木賞，両方とれるか？

A: Who was it that won the previous Akutagawa Prize—Shimatani Katsuhito?

B:（2. 彼がその賞を受賞したはずは全くないよ）.

A: Why not?

B: Because he got the Naoki Prize three years ago. No single writer is ever awarded both of those prizes.

　　2. (won / possibly / that / he / have / prize / couldn't)

....

Dialogue C　本当に人気レストランなのか？

A: This restaurant is said to be crowded every night, but so far this evening you and I are the only customers.

B: Maybe the restaurant itself somehow created a rumor about its great popularity.

A: I don't know, but (2. たしかに, 前もって予約をする必要なんてなかったようだね).

3. (needn't / it / beforehand / certainly looks / we / have / a reservation / like / made)

....

 ## 3 Focus on Grammar

文法を理解しよう

★ 助動詞＋have＋過去分詞形

(Q&A)

Q1 次のうち, 誤りのある文を 1 つ指摘せよ.

(1) He may be in Kyoto now.

(2) He may return soon.

(3) He may meet Meg last night.

Q2 次の 2 文のうち, どちらがその下に示されている和訳に対応する英文として適切か.

(1) He can have stolen my purse.

(2) He could have stolen my purse.

彼が私の財布を盗んだ可能性がある.

Q3 must のように過去形を持たない助動詞を用いて, 過去のことを「～した［だった］に違いない」と推量をする場合はどうするか.

Q4 同じ〈助動詞＋have＋過去分詞形〉でも, 以下の 2 文は「過去のことに対する推量」ではない. どのような内容を表しているか.

① He would have finished the task by now.

② He will have finished the work by tomorrow morning.

A1 (3)

・助動詞を用いて過去のことを推量するには〈助動詞 ＋ have ＋過去分詞形〉という型にする. つまり (2) は He may <u>have met</u> Meg last night. とする必要がある.

A2 (2)

・〈助動詞 ＋ have ＋過去分詞形〉という型を用いて過去のことを推量する際には, 助動詞は過去形で用いられることが多い. 過去の可能性について,「～した［だった］はずがない」と推量する場合は〈cannot have 過去分詞形〉と〈couldn't have 過去分詞形〉

のいずれを用いることもできるが，「〜した［だった］可能性がある」という肯定の意味の場合は〈could have 過去分詞形〉のみを用いる。また，過去のことを will を用いて推量する場合は，必ず would を用いる。つまり〈would have 過去分詞形〉あるいは〈wouldn't have 過去分詞形〉という形になる。

・may は現在形だが，例外的にこの型で頻繁に用いられる。つまり過去のことについて「〜した［だった］かもしれない」と推量する場合は，〈may have 過去分詞形〉と〈might have 過去分詞形〉の両方が広く用いられる。

A3 そのまま must を用いて〈must have 過去分詞形〉とする。

A4 ①は現在完了の内容に対して推量を加えている。

②はいわゆる「未来完了」。未来時の「完了」について推量を加えている。

例文

① He may have come here last night.

② Lisa might have been rich when she had the business.

③ You should have helped him more.

④ You shouldn't have drunk so much yesterday.

⑤ I ought to have accepted your offer.

⑥ You ought not to have eaten that piece of cake.

⑦ How could you believe he would have done such a thing?

⑧ I still think she wouldn't have wanted to answer the question.

⑨ You could have won the game more easily.

⑩ You cannot have been there at that time yesterday.

⑪ She couldn't have met her father at noon today.

⑫ He must have been busy last week.

⑬ You needn't have come here yesterday.

⑭ All of them may have died by now.

⑮ He will have received the letter before you reach there.

解説

■ ①② 〈may have 過去分詞形〉〈might have 過去分詞形〉が用いられた文。might を用いたほうが控えめな推量となる。

■ ③④ 〈should have 過去分詞形〉〈shouldn't have 過去分詞形〉が用いられた文。前者は「〜すべきだった」，後者は「すべきでなかった」の意。

- ■ ⑤⑥　should と同意の ought to が用いられた文。否定表現は ought not to となることに注意。not は ought と to の間にはさむ。

- ■ ⑦⑧　〈would have 過去分詞形〉は「～した［だった］だろう」の意。意志のニュアンスが入ることも多い〈wouldn't have 過去分詞形〉はその否定表現。これらの表現では, will は用いない。

- ■ ⑨　〈could have 過去分詞形〉は過去の可能性の推量。この場合に can を用いることは不可。

- ■ ⑩⑪　〈couldn't [can't] have 過去分詞形〉は, 過去の可能性の推量（否定）。つまり「～した［だった］はすがない〉の意。could がより好まれる。

- ■ ⑫　〈must have 過去分詞形〉は「～した［だった］に違いない, きっと～だったのだろう」の意。

- ■ ⑬　〈needn't have 過去分詞形〉は, 過去の“不必要”について述べる表現。つまり「～する必要はなかった」の意。

- ■ ⑭　述語部分が〈助動詞＋have＋過去分詞形〉の形だが, by now から過去のことに対する推量ではないとわかる。これは現在完了の内容について may で推量を加えている文。

- ■ ⑮　before you reach there で未来時が設定されているので, いわゆる「未来完了」の例。

4 Exercises

次の文を指定された語数で英訳しましょう。（　　　）内で示されている語は必要に応じて, 形を変えたうえで用いてください。

① 私たちはもっと大きな車を買うべきだった。（7 語／ big）

　　...

② 君はその腕時計を売るべきではなかった。（6 語）

　　...

③ 彼は昨晩そこにいたはずがない。（7 語）
　　※ night で文を終える

　　...

④ 君は地図を持ってくる必要はなかった。（6 語）

....

⑤ 彼女はそう言ったのかもしれない。（5 語）

....

⑥ 彼は今頃は空港に着いているに違いない。（9 語／ arrive）

....

⑦ 私たちは来週の終わりまでにこの仕事を完遂しているだろう。
　　　　　　　　　　　（13 語／ probably, complete, work）※ week で文を終える

....

⑧ 彼はその事件の後，しばらくの間はその部屋に留まっていたに違いない。
　　　　　　　　　　　（13 語／ stay, a while, incident）※ incident で文を終える

....

⑨ 君は自分がもっといい成績を取ることができたと思わないか。（9 語／ get, grade）

....

⑩ 彼女は昨日からあそこで働いているかもしれない。（8 語）

....

CHAPTER 12
仮定法の壁を超えよう！

この章では，現実ではないことを想定する，いわゆる「仮定法過去」「仮定法過去完了」に焦点をあてます。難しいイメージがあり敬遠されがちですが，日常的に英語を話すうえで不可欠な表現です。

1 *Opening Monologue* ▷▷▷ 私は生まれていなかったかもしれない…

★ 下線を引いた文に注意し，表現を覚えよう

Today is a Sunday, and the weather is absolutely wonderful. <u>If I didn't have so much homework left to do, I would go out right now and do some cycling, which I really love.</u> A lot of the professors at my school are especially strict when it comes to giving out credit, and if you miss a few classes, you can easily find yourself having to repeat a year. Actually, though, I think it's probably good for me to be ⁵ reined in like that, and, in any case, it looks as if I'll be at my desk studying for most of the day today.

Outside the window, I can see my father doing a little yard work. Unlike myself, who loves playing all kinds of sports, my father is an indoor type. When he was young, he wanted to be a writer, and I once read a very interesting mystery story ¹⁰ that he had written when he was still in college. <u>If he hadn't gone to work for a company and had continued to pursue his passion for writing, I think he might have become a famous author.</u> But, then again, it was at his company that he met my mother, which resulted in my being born. <u>In other words, if he had actually chosen to follow that dream of his youth, I wouldn't even exist in the world right now.</u> ¹⁵

This is the season for picking cucumbers and eggplant in our vegetable garden. I'm looking forward to having some fresh vegetables for lunch today, and this morning I'll try to get two assignments done before then.

NOTES ————

3– **when it comes to ~**「~ということになると，~に関しては」／ 6 **rein in**「制御する，抑制する」／ 12 **pursue**「追い求める」

2 # *Understanding More Variations*

次の英文を読み，（　　　）内の和訳を参考に，英単語を並べ替えてみよう。なお，文頭に置かれる語は大文字で始めてください。

Dialogue A　百獣の王はどの動物か？

A: The African lion is often called the "King of Beasts," which makes it sound terribly dangerous.

B: That's true. (1. まるでライオンが，ほかのどんな動物よりも人間にとって危険であるかのようだね) in Africa.

A: Isn't that so?

B: Actually, no. Hippopotamuses kill more people in Africa than lions or any other mammal, and venomous snakes are even more deadly, but mosquitos are by far the most dangerous animal for Africans—simply because of the many serious diseases that they spread.

　1. (to / posed / it's / lions / any other / more of / humans / than / a danger / animal / as if)

....

● **NOTES**
pose「〜を引き起こす，〜となる」／ **hippopotamus**「カバ」／ **mammal**「哺乳類，哺乳動物」／ **venomous**「毒をもつ」

Dialogue B　コーランを原典で読みたい

A: Lately, I've become interested in Islam. I'd like to read the Koran in the original language.

B: Because the Koran is that religion's "sacred scripture"?

A: Yes. (2. アラビア語が読めればなあ). I want to start learning it.

B: It's said to be a particularly difficult language to learn, but I definitely think you should try.

　2. (read / wish / I / Arabic / could / I)

....

● **NOTES**
sacred scripture「経典，聖なる書物」

Dialogue C 金貨を買っておけばよかった

A: Some years ago, I saw a set of solidus coins on an Internet site, but the price was over ¥100,000, which seemed too expensive for me at the time, and I didn't buy it.

B: I learned about those gold coins in my World History class. I think they were first created in the Late Roman Empire period.

A: That's right, and the set on sale was particularly old. I wish I *had* bought it. (3. もし買っておけば, いい投資になったはずだ) —the set would be many times more valuable now than what I would have paid for it back then.

3. (investment / a / had / it / would / if / have / I / bought / good / been / it)

....

● **NOTES**

solidus「ソリダス。古代ローマ帝国の金貨」

 Focus on Grammar

文法を理解しよう

★ 仮定法

(Q&A)

Q1 〈if SV（現在形）〉と〈if SV（過去形）〉では, どのような意味の違いがあるだろうか。

Q2 過去の事実をふまえたうえで,「（事実に反して）もし～だったら, …だっただろう」ということを述べる場合, if 節の述語の形と, 主節の述語の形はどうなるだろうか。

Q3 過去の事実をふまえたうえで,「（事実に反して）もし～だったら, 今頃は…だろう」ということを述べる場合, if 節の述語の形と, 主節の述語の形はどうなるだろうか。

Q4 I wish (that) I am a bird.（私は自分が鳥であることを願う→自分が鳥ならなぁ）という文を正しい形に改めよ。

Q5 「（あたかも）SV のようだ」を意味する表現である〈as if [though] SV〉を用いる際に, V の形はどうなるか。

Q6 次の2文はどのような意味の違いがあるか。

① It's time we stand up for our rights.

② It's time we stood up for our rights.

A1 現実味のあることについての仮定は〈if SV（現在形）〉を用いる。また，可能性がわからない場合もこの形を用いる。

一方，可能性が低い場合，あるいは現実ではないことについて述べる場合は〈if SV（過去形）〉を用いる。この述語の形を仮定法過去という。

・仮定法過去を受ける主節（帰結節）の述語は〈助動詞（過去形）＋動詞（原形）〉という形になる。助動詞を過去形で用いることに注意。帰結節で用いられる助動詞は，主に would, could, might である。

・仮定法過去においては，if 節に be 動詞を用いる場合，主語が単数のものである場合や不可算名詞である場合でも，were を用いるのが正しいが，was も多用される。

A2 if 節の内側の述語は過去完了形，つまり〈had ＋動詞（過去分詞形）〉となる（この述語の形を「仮定法過去完了」という）。受ける主節の述語は〈助動詞（過去形）＋ have ＋動詞（過去分詞形）〉という形になる。

A3 if 節の述語は過去完了形となり，主節は〈助動詞（過去形）＋動詞（原形）〉という形になる。

A4 I wish (that) I were a bird.

・wish に (that) SV が後続する場合で，wish の前に置かれる主語と，(that) SV の S が一致する場合は，wish は儚い願い（可能性の低い願い）について述べるので，V は仮定法となる。以下の基準で用いる。

・wish の時点と，願っている内容にズレがない場合

→ V は過去形となる。

・今より過去（あるいは過去の時点よりも更に過去）の現実をふまえたうえで，「（事実に反して）〜だったならなぁ」と述べる場合

→ V は過去完了形となる。

A5 内容に現実味があれば，現在形を用いる。現実味がない場合や，現実のことでない場合は，V は過去形となる。現在より過去（あるいは過去の時点よりも更に過去）の現実をふまえたうえで「本当はそうでなかったが，あたかも〜であったかのように」という内容を述べる場合は，V は過去完了形となる。

A6 ①は単に「〜する時だ」と述べている文だが，②は仮定法過去を用いることにより，非現実であることを突きつけて，「まだ現実になってないじゃないか → 早くしなきゃ」というように，せきたてる感じが出ている。

① If I won a lottery, I would buy a car.

② If I became a doctor, I could take care of them.

③ If you could talk to animals, what would you say to them?

④ If we were living without smartphones, we would be bored.

⑤ If you had helped him, he would have succeeded.

⑥ I might have chosen this one if I had seen it first.

⑦ If you hadn't helped me then, I wouldn't be alive now.

⑧ We wish we lived in a utopian society.

⑨ I wish I hadn't said that.

⑩ She often looks as if she has a headache.

⑪ I behaved as if I didn't know anything.

⑫ He behaved as if he had seen an alien.

⑬ It's time you changed your behavior.

⑭ It's about time you got up.

⑮ It's high time you finished your homework.

解説

■ ①②③④　仮定法過去が用いられた文。②以外では，帰結節の助動詞に would が用いられている。「もし〜なら」ではなく，「もし〜できるなら」という内容を表す場合は，③のように if 節の内側に could が置かれる。「もし〜するなら」ではなく，「もし〜しているなら」という進行の内容を表す場合は，④のように〈if S be 動詞（過去形）doing〉という形になる。

■ ⑤⑥　仮定法過去完了が用いられた文。⑥では if 節が後半に置かれている。

■ ⑦　「もし（過去の時点で）〜だったら，今頃は…はずだ」という内容の文。

■ ⑧⑨　〈S wish (that) S V〉の型。⑧は V が過去形なので，願っている時と願っている内容が同じ時点。⑨は V が過去完了形なので，過去のことについて願っている。

■ ⑩⑪⑫　as if 節が用いられた文。⑩は as if 節内の動詞が現在形なので，現実味があると考えている。⑪は as if 節内の動詞が過去形なので，behaved と同じ時点のことについて「本当はそうではないが，あたかも〜」という内容を述べている。一方で⑫は，as if 節内の動詞が過去完了形なので，behaved の時点よりも前のことについて述べている。

■ ⑬⑭⑮　「そろそろ〜する時間だ」という内容の文。time の後ろの SV の V が過去形なので，せきたてるように述べている。time の前に，⑪のように about（そろそろ），⑫のように high（とっくに）が置かれることもある。

4 Exercises

次の文を指定された語数で英訳しましょう。①〜④, ⑩は英文を if で始め, (　　)
内で示されている語は必要に応じて, 形を変えたうえで用いてください。

① もし私が彼の住所を知っていたら, 彼に手紙を書く。(10 語)

....

② もし私がドイツ語をしゃべれるなら, このエッセイを理解できるはずだ。(10 語)

....

③ もし私がきのう忙しかったら, 彼女を助けることができなかったはずだ。(11 語)

....

④ もしあなたがあの時, 彼の提案を受け入れていれば, 今は金持ちになっているはずだ。
(14 語／ proposal, that)

....

⑤ 彼はまるでプロの歌手であるかのように歌う。(9 語)

....

⑥ 君みたいにハンサムならなあ！ (7 語)

....

⑦ あの腕時計を買っておけばなあ。(7 語)

....

⑧ 君はとっくに中国語を学び始める時だよ！ (8 語／ high, start)

....

⑨ 彼女は何度もロンドンに行ったことがあるかのような口ぶりだった。

（11 語／ talk, be to）

....

⑩ もし彼に十分な時間が与えられていたら，彼はその仕事を完遂していたはずだ。

（13 語／ give, complete, job）

....

CHAPTER 13
使いこなせると便利な同格表現

英語には，2つ以上の名詞（もしくは名詞あるいは形容詞の役割をもつ句や節）を並べて，後ろにある語が前の語を説明する同格表現と呼ばれるものがあります。より複雑な内容を話したり書いたりするときに必須の用法を学びましょう。

1 Opening Dialogue ▷▷▷▷▷▷ 就職活動，ついに終わりました！

★ 下線を引いた文に注意し，表現を覚えよう

Kumi: Where will you be working?

Shinji: Mitsui Motors.

Kumi: Fantastic! That was your first choice!

Shinji: It was, and I'm really happy about it. I definitely wanted to get into something related to car manufacturing. 5

Kumi: I'm very happy for you. It's wonderful that you'll be able to work at a such a major international automaker. I don't know much about cars, but the Japanese auto industry is the best in the world, isn't it?

Shinji: Well, *I* think it is. <u>Cars from Europe and the U.S. are great, and some emerging countries are catching up fast, but there's no denying the fact that the 10 Japanese industry is still the best in the world overall.</u>

Kumi: That's what I thought.

Shinji: Where will you be working? I imagine in an architectural design office.

Kumi: That's right. I want to design buildings, and I've been accepted at the company that I most hoped to be able to work for. 15

Shinji: Great! You've always had a true passion for architecture. <u>I have a feeling that you'll be a great success as an architect.</u>

Kumi: Thanks!

Shinji: What do you think it was that got you accepted?

Kumi: I'm not sure. But during my interview, we had a lot of fun talking excitedly 20 about historical buildings in Tokyo.

Shinji: It's always a good sign when an interview seems to be going along smoothly and enjoyably.

Kumi: That's true. But, when I went in for mine, I had no intention of trying to create any sort of lively discussion. 25

Shinji: Still, that's what it turned into, probably because at heart you've always been so sincerely devoted to the study of architecture.

Kumi: Maybe so.

Shinji: In any case, I'm really glad that we've both got what we hoped for in our job hunting. 30

Kumi: So am I. And I'm feeling tremendously relieved, too.

NOTES ———————

10 **emerging countries**「新興国」／ 24 **go in for**「〈試験などを〉受ける」／ 31 **tremendously**「ものすごく，途方もなく」

 ## 2 *Understanding More Variations*

次の英文を読み，（　　　　）内の和訳を参考に，英単語を並べ替えてみよう。なお，文頭に置かれる語は大文字で始めてください。

Dialogue A　ネット社会における表現の自由とは？

A: In countries like Japan,（1. ネット上にほとんど何でも好きなことを書き込む自由がある）, but I sometimes wonder whether or not that is really a good thing.

B: There *is* a lot of misinformation and disinformation on the net, as well as terribly hurtful personal attacks and cyberbullying.

A: There certainly is. There probably should be some sort of regulation to try to stop that.

B: I agree, but it seems nearly impossible to impose meaningful restrictions while, at the same time, still preserving the right of free speech guaranteed by the Constitution.

1. (want to / on / to / almost anything / people / the freedom / write / the Internet / they / have)

....

Dialogue B ポーランド第2の都市クラクフの魅力

A: I visited Poland during the summer vacation. The country's second largest city, Kraków, was enchanting and much more enjoyable than Warsaw, Poland's capital.

B: I've heard that there are wonderful examples of medieval and renaissance architecture remaining in Kraków's historic center.

A: Yes, but, unfortunately, the same cannot be said for Warsaw. (2. それ［ワルシャワ］は第二次世界大戦のときに，ほとんど完全に破壊されてしまったという悲しい歴史を持っている). Some historic buildings have been reconstructed, but most of the city's architecture is modern.

2. (World War II / it / destroyed / history of / suffers / the / having / been / almost entirely / from / sad / during)

....

....

● **NOTES**
enchanting「魅力的な」

Dialogue C 5月が大好きです

A: You seem to be looking rather cheerful.

B: It's May, and (3. 私は5月という月が大好きでね)! I always feel buoyed up this time of year.

A: I recently saw the results of a survey that said the most popular months among Japanese people were April, May, and October.

B: Those are definitely the most pleasant of all, aren't they?

3. (the / May / love / just / of / month / I)

....

● **NOTES**
buoyed up「〈気分などが〉高揚した」

3 ## *Focus on Grammar*

文法を理解しよう

★同格表現

Q&A

Q1 たとえば news のように,「誰がどうした?」「何がどうする?」という内容を含む名詞を用いて,「誰がどうしたというニュース」「何がどうするというニュース」という内容を表現したい場合,内容の部分はどのような形にしたうえで,どの位置に置くか。

Q2 たとえば He made a decision. という文の decision からは,「どうするという決心?」という疑問が生じる。同様に He has a habit. という文の habit からは,「何をする癖?」という疑問が生じる。Q1 で見た通り,news からは「誰がどうした?」「何がどうする?」という疑問が生じるが,decision, habit のように,下線部の情報(主語の情報)は不要で,単に「どうする?」「何をする?」という内容のみを名詞に後続させる際には,どのような形を用いるか。

Q3 名詞に対する説明となる語(同格語)には,他にどのような形のものがあるか。

A1 that 節にして名詞の後ろに置く。

・この that 節(「同格の that 節」という)を和訳する際には,必要に応じて「という」「との」などの言葉を補う。

・同格の that 節が後続する代表的な名詞は,多くの英和辞典にその旨の記載がある。たとえば news や fact などには〈that 節〉などの表記があることが多い。

A2 〈to do〉か〈of doing〉を後続させるのが基本。その前の名詞によって〈for doing〉や〈in doing〉あるいは〈at doing〉などを用いることもある。

・これらは準動詞句を用いた同格表現である。どの形を用いるかは名詞ごとに異なる。代表的な名詞に関しては,英和辞典に,どの形を取るかの記載があることが多い。たとえば decision には〈to do〉という表記があり,habit には〈of+doing〉という表記(あるいは単に of の表記)があることが多い。

・これらの表現を和訳するにも,必要に応じて「という」「との」などの言葉を補う。

A3 〈of + 名詞〉や,言い換えの名詞。

・of + 名詞を和訳する際には,必要に応じて「という」「との」などの言葉を補う。

例文

① Did you hear the news that Lisa is getting married?

② There is no evidence that she is guilty.

③ The possibility that he would succeed as a pitcher was lost forever.

④ He may not have meant it, but the fact remains that he committed a crime.

⑤ I was rather surprised at his decision to leave this team.

⑥ You have no right to state your opinion.

⑦ The heart has the function of pumping blood throughout the body.

⑧ I never thought about the danger of being arrested.

⑨ There is no method for curing this disease.

⑩ Her skill in [at] managing documents is superior to the majority of her rivals.

⑪ I heard he is from the city of Denver.

⑫ The game of chess is played all over the world.

⑬ He is Robert Smith, President of this university.

⑭ She graduated from Waseda, one of the best-known universities in Japan.

解説

■ ①②③④　同格の that 節が用いられた文。①②④では和訳の際に，that 節に「という」「との」，あるいは口語では「って」などの言葉を補う。③は逆に補うと不自然になる。④は that 節の位置に注意。〈S +同格の that 節 + V …〉という構造においては，この文のように，that 節 (that he commited a crime) が文末に移動することが多い（このことは S を修飾する関係詞節にもあてはまる）。

■ ⑤⑥⑦⑧　同格の準動詞句が用いられた表現。同格語として⑤⑥は〈to do〉，⑦⑧は〈of + doing〉が用いられた形。この 2 つの形が同格の準動詞句のメインの用法だといえる。

■ ⑨⑩　⑨は同格語として for + doing が用いられた形。「～する技術」は，⑩のように skill に対して in doing, at doing のいずれもが後続しうる。

■ ⑪⑫　同格の内容が〈of + 名詞〉で示されているもの。the city of Denver は「デンバーという都市」と訳し，the game of chess は「チェスというゲーム」と訳す。

■ ⑬⑭　〈名詞 1 + 名詞 2〉という並びで，名詞 2 が名詞 1 の言い換え，説明になっているという構造が見られる文。⑬では Robert Smith と President of this university が，それぞれ名詞 1 と名詞 2 に当たる。⑭では Waseda と one of the best-known universities in Japan が名詞 1 と名詞 2 に当たる。

 **Exercises**

次の文を指定された語数で英訳しましょう。（　　　　　）内で示されている語は必要に応じて，形を変えたうえで用いてください。

① 彼は妻が入院中だという噂を否定した。（10 語または 11 語）

....

② 私たちは浩二が日本で最高の歌手だという結論に達した。（13 語／ come）

....

③ 私にはそのドアを開ける勇気がなかった。（9 語）

....

④ 私の夫はベッドではタバコを吸わないという約束を破った。（10 語）

....

⑤ 彼には頭を振る癖がある。（8 語）

....

⑥ なぜ彼女はあんなにも深く横浜という都市を愛しているのだろうか。（10 語／ that）

....

⑦ これはアメリカの 37 代目の大統領であったリチャード・ニクソンの肖像画だ。（13 語）

....

⑧ 私は 2 人の子供を育てる経済的な負担を軽くしたかった。
（11 語／ wish, ease, financial, burden, raise）

....

⑨ 全時代を通して最も有名な野球選手であるベーブ・ルースについて聞いたことがあります
か。 （14 語／ about, time）

....

⑩ 彼がいま生きている可能性はどれくらいだろうか。（9 語／ what, probability, alive）

....

2つ以上の単語で1つの前置詞ができる!?

because of, in spite of, at the risk of のように，2つ以上の単語を組み合わせて、前置詞と同じ働きになる表現があります。「群前置詞」と呼ばれるこれらの用法について考えてみましょう。

1 **Opening Dialogue** ▷▷▷▷▷▷ うちの学食は日本一

★ 下線を引いた文に注意し，表現を覚えよう

Kenji: The food at our school cafeteria is really good, isn't it?

Mami: It's the greatest. I seriously think we have the best school cafeteria in Japan.

Kenji: You think so, too? That's what I've always thought.

Mami: A lot of people from outside the university also seem to come to eat here.

Kenji: That's right. They come just for the food. But I guess I can understand that— 5
all the dishes served here are delicious.

Mami: But I wonder how the cooking came to be so good.

Kenji: I wondered about that, too, and I once asked one of the lunch ladies about it.

Mami: What did she say?

Kenji: According to her, the chief chef is a true master of his trade. She said that he 10
worked for very many years in charge of kitchens in all sorts of restaurants—
French, Italian, Japanese.

Mami: Really!

Kenji: Then, she said, after he retired from that, he felt that he wanted more young
people to experience the pleasures of good food, and he started working here. 15
Look! There he is, coming out of the kitchen right now!

Mami: That man? We're lucky to have him, aren't we? Thanks to him, we can enjoy
great lunches every day.

Kenji: That's right. But in contrast to this cafeteria, the eating places around the
station all seem to leave just a bit to be desired, don't they? 20

Mami: Well, most of them do, I guess, but I *have* heard of a really nice new bistro.

2つ以上の単語で1つの前置詞ができる!?　**83**

Kenji: Where is it?

Mami: <u>Next to the Yūhi Plaza Hotel.</u> <u>In front of Fureai Square.</u>

Kenji: Who told you about it?

Mami: Yumika.

Kenji: If *she* says it's nice, then it must be.

Mami: Let's try it out sometime soon.

Kenji: How about if we go there for our club's next end-of-season party?

Mami: That sounds good. Let's do it.

NOTES ————

8 **lunch lady**「学校などの公共施設で食事を提供する女性スタッフ」／ 20 **leave just a bit to be desired**「ちょっとだけ物足りないところがある」

2 **Understanding More Variations**

次の英文を読み，（　　　）内の和訳を参考に，英単語を並べ替えてみよう。なお，文頭に置かれる語は大文字で始めてください。

Dialogue A 本当の天才とは？

A: You really have an amazing talent as a conductor. It's absolute genius!

B: Not at all. (1. 天才からは程遠いですよ). "Genius" means the talent of conductors like Furtwängler and Toscanini.

A: They *are* both legendary. I seem to remember that Furtwängler was German, but what was Toscanini?

B: He was Italian.

1. (very / it's / far / of genius / from / the level)

....

Dialogue B やる気次第で英語の達人になれる

A: It seems that there were a lot of Japanese people in the Meiji period who were highly accomplished at English.

B: And some of them managed to become truly excellent speakers of the language (2. 音声教材という点では，当時はほとんど何もなかったという事実にもかかわらず).

A: I think they must have succeeded simply as a result of the very hard work they put in, striving doggedly as they did to help Japan catch up with the West. People who study with true determination are bound to get results.

B: Maybe we should reflect on the way we've been studying.

2. (there was / spite of / that / audio / little / in the way of / teaching / back then / the fact / materials / in)

....

....

● NOTES
doggedly「根気強く」

Dialogue C　オオカミがいなくなった理由

A: There used to be wolves in Japan.

B: That's right—the "Japanese wolf."

A: But they seem to have gone extinct sometime early in the 20th century, (3. 1つには ジステンパーや狂犬病のような新種の病気のため，1つには絶滅させようという政府の政策のために).

B: Even so, some people still occasionally claim to have sighted a surviving wolf, though no convincing evidence has ever been produced.

3. (new diseases / a government policy / partly because / of extermination / of / and partly because / distemper and rabies, / of / like)

....

....

● NOTES
rabies「狂犬病」

3 Focus on Grammar

文法を理解しよう

★群前置詞

Q&A

Q1 以下の文に 1 語を加えて正しい文にせよ。

The game was canceled because rain.

(その試合は雨のために中止になった)

Q2 群前置詞句の主な文法上のはたらきはどのようなものか。つまり，S，V，C，O，修飾語のいずれとしてはたらくか。そして修飾語である場合は，どの品詞を修飾するか。

Q3 以下の文の下線部のそれぞれの語の品詞は何か。

A cat appeared <u>from</u> <u>behind</u> the curtain.

(そのカーテンの後ろからネコが現れた)

A1 The game was canceled because <u>of</u> rain.

・because には前置詞としての用法がない。後ろに SV…ではなく，名詞を置くには because of とする。この句は 2 語で事実上の前置詞として機能している。このようなものを「群前置詞」という。群前置詞は，ほとんどのものが 2 語〜 4 語で構成される。

・群前置詞の後ろに置かれる名詞は，「群前置詞の目的語」である。

・〈群前置詞＋群前置詞の目的語〉のセットを「群前置詞句」という。

A2 動詞に対する修飾語として用いられることが最も多い。他にも名詞に対する修飾語，C などとしても用いられる。

・A1 の例でも，because of rain のまとまりが動詞 was canceled を修飾している。

A3 from も behind も前置詞。

・from behind は「二重前置詞」の一例。二重前置詞は，群前置詞のように「まとめて 1 つの前置詞」ととらえるのではなく，2 つの前置詞それぞれに意味を読み込む。

・二重前置詞は，「名詞→前置詞 2 →前置詞 1」の順に，後ろから和訳する。

例文

①He was unable to complete the job because of illness.

②He was walking ahead of me.

③There was a tall man sitting next to me.

④He couldn't go there for fear of death.

⑤In addition to determination, an actor must have fine acting skills to survive.

⑥ In spite of her beauty, she was very timid.

⑦ He succeeded in the face of many difficulties.

⑧ He worked hard at the risk of his health.

⑨ The man in front of the gate was Jack.

⑩ This mistake is due to her carelessness.

⑪ The new president was chosen from among the employees.

⑫ I've been here since before you were born.

解説

- ■ ①②③　2 語の群前置詞 (because of, ahead of, next to) が用いられた文。いずれも群前置詞句は，動詞を修飾している。

- ■ ④⑤⑥　3 語の群前置詞 (for fear of, in addition to, in spite of) が用いられた文。いずれも群前置詞句は，動詞を修飾している。

- ■ ⑦⑧　4 語の群前置詞句 (in the face of, at the risk of) が用いられた文。いずれも群前置詞句は，動詞を修飾している。

- ■ ⑨　群前置詞句が名詞を修飾している例。in front of the gate が man を修飾している。

- ■ ⑩　This mistake が S，is が V，群前置詞句の due to her carelessness が C という構造の文。

- ■ ⑪⑫　二重前置詞が用いられた文。from among, since before の部分が二重前置詞。

4　Exercises

次の文を指定された語数で英訳しましょう。（　　　　　）内で示されている語は必要に応じて，形を変えたうえで用いてください。

① 彼はその部屋から駆け出した。（6 語／ rush）

....

② 私たちは大雪のために車で家まで帰れなかった。（8 語）

....

③ 年齢に関係なくこのゲームは楽しめますよ。(9 語／ regardless)

....

④ うちの息子は 100 まで数えられる。(7 語)

....

⑤ 火災の場合は，このボタンを押しなさい。(7 語または 8 語)

....

⑥ この成功は君のサポートのお蔭だ。(7 語／ thanks)

....

⑦ カーテンの後ろから犬が現れた。(7 語)

....

⑧ 大雨にもかかわらず，その野外コンサートは予定通りに開かれた。
(12 語または 13 語／ as)　※ scheduled で文を終える

....

⑨ 彼らは自分たちの税を払うのに，銀の代わりに塩を使った。(10 語／ instead)
※ taxes で文を終える

....

⑩ その机の下から一匹の美しいネコが現れた。(8 語／ appear)　※ desk で文を終える

....

CHAPTER 15
前置詞 *before* や *after* の後に来るものとは？

「前置詞のあとには，名詞や名詞に準じるものが置かれる」というルールは意外に守られないことが多いようです。英語の基本事項で，会話，作文に頻出する，この用法をぜひ押さえておきましょう。

1 *Opening Dialogue* ▷▷▷▷▷▷ 紙の辞書のすばらしさ

★ 下線を引いた文に注意し，表現を覚えよう

Kaori: Dad, where's today's English-language newspaper?

Tohru: Here it is. I was reading it just now in my den.

Kaori: Thanks. But, you know, it's such a bother having to look words up in a dictionary whenever I try to read articles. <u>I wish I could read English without using a dictionary.</u> 5

Tohru: But you have an electronic dictionary, which makes it so much less work. When I was a student, we only had print dictionaries.

Kaori: <u>Looking up words by paging through a book is really time-consuming, isn't it?</u> I hate that sort of inefficiency.

Tohru: I can understand that, but on the paper pages of a print dictionary, you can 10 underline things and make notes in the margins. <u>By doing that, you can add to the book's value as a reference work for yourself personally.</u>

Kaori: I suppose you *do* have a point there.

Tohru: Also, people often come to feel, over the years, a sense of attachment, even a certain affection, for their well-worn print dictionaries. That's something you're 15 not likely to find with electronic dictionaries.

Kaori: That's for sure. If I were to lose my electronic dictionary, it would definitely be a *financial* blow, but I wouldn't feel anything at all *emotionally*.

Tohru: A dictionary printed on paper in book form can have a kind of warmth to it. Also, you can think of it as a book for just reading, too. <u>In paging through one,</u> 20 <u>you can make all kinds of interesting discoveries about words, and you can gain</u>

knowledge about other things—like people and places—as well.

Kaori: That wouldn't be very easy to do with an electronic dictionary, would it?

Tohru: No, it wouldn't. As a learning tool, a print dictionary is not necessarily *completely* inefficient.   25

Kaori: I guess not.

Tohru: And that's not the only case of something's being lost with people's simply emphasizing ease of use rather than taking into account the whole range of possibly important factors.

Kaori: What are some other examples?   30

Tohru: Think about the use of CDs and music-streaming services, as opposed to playing vinyl records, for instance.

Kaori: I've never played any vinyl records, but it seems like it would be a lot of work.

Tohru: It certainly can be, but the quality of the analog sound from vinyl is especially warm and pleasing.   35

Kaori: I *have* heard that some people prefer it over digital.

Tohru: That's right. A lot of people have discovered, or rediscovered, the warmth of analog, and vinyl has been making a fairly big comeback.

Kaori: Maybe print dictionaries will make a comeback, too.

Tohru: That would be nice.   40

NOTES ────────

2 **den**「(小さい) 書斎, 仕事部屋」 ／ 9 **inefficiency**「非効率」 ／ 15 **well-worn**「使いこまれた」 ／ 18 **blow**「(精神的なものも含む) 打撃」

2 *Understanding More Variations*

次の英文を読み,（　　　）内の和訳を参考に，英単語を並べ替えてみよう。なお，文頭に置かれる語は大文字で始めてください。

Dialogue A　英文多読の前に必要なこと

A: They say that extensive reading is especially important to any effort to learn English. I'd like to do that, but I don't want to just jump into it haphazardly.

B: Of course not. And it won't be of much help if you don't actually understand what you're reading.（1. どんな多読の計画に進む前でも，しっかりとした文法の理解が必要です）.

A: I guess so. I'd better do some serious grammar study first.

1. (before / yourself / you / immersing /get / of grammar /need to / in any extensive reading project / a really solid grasp)

....

....

●NOTES
haphazardly「無計画に，やみくもに」

Dialogue B　消防士のプライド

A: Last night at a bar, I happened to be seated at the counter next to a firefighter, and I talked a little with him.

B: Did you enjoy that?

A: Yes. He was a light-hearted, sociable kind of guy. But when the conversation turned to his work, he suddenly got extremely serious. And（2. 彼は自分が消防士であることに大きな誇りをもっているのだなって強く感じたよ）.

B: He must have to deal with injuries and death all the time. That kind of work requires a strong sense of mission and a willingness to risk one's own life. Anyone who does it deserves our respect.

2. (being / was / I / a firefighter / that / he / very proud / strongly felt / of)

....

●NOTES
light-hearted「陽気な，面白い」

Dialogue C　戦前の義務教育

A: Did you know that in pre-war Japan compulsory education only went up to elementary school?

B: I *did* know that. My great-grandfather only got an elementary school education.

A: I guess that much schooling was thought to be enough for most people.

B: Back then, even though you might have wanted to go on to the next level, if your family wasn't especially well off, it was likely that budget considerations would mean（3. 上の学校に行くかわりに働くことを余儀なくされた）.

3. (have to /of / work / instead / go to / your education / you'd / furthering)

....

3 Focus on Grammar

文法を理解しよう

★前置詞／群前置詞＋動名詞

Q&A

Q1 前置詞の後ろに動詞を含む内容を置きたい場合は，動詞はどのような形になるか。

Q2 before は接続詞だろうか，それとも前置詞だろうか。

Q3 群前置詞の後ろに動詞を含む内容を置きたい場合は，動詞はどのような形になるか。

A1 ing 形，つまり動名詞となる。

A2 接続詞かつ前置詞である。

・第 14 章で扱った because は「接続詞のみ」であり，前置詞として用いるには because of という形になったが，before, after, until, till, since などは，両方の品詞として用いることができる。

A3 動名詞となる。

・前置詞の場合と同じ。

例文

① Can you read this book without using a dictionary?

② Joe killed time by watching a movie on his tablet.

③ You must take off your shoes before entering the room.

④ English ability is often very important in dealing with customers from abroad.

⑤ On hearing the sound, the dog ran away.

⑥ She succeeded in opening the box.

⑦ I have failed in achieving my goal.

⑧ He objected to my buying a car.

⑨ I am satisfied with being a teacher at this school.

⑩ I am interested in my students' learning how to have everyday conversations in English.

⑪ When did you get interested in playing the guitar?

⑫ Instead of going abroad, I stayed in Milwaukee.

⑬ He was in the habit of drinking alone at night.

■ ①②③④⑤ 〈前置詞＋動名詞〉という連なりが存在する文。④の in doing は「〜することにおいて，〜する際に」という意味。⑤の on doing は「〜して，〜するや否や」という意味。

■ ⑥⑦⑧ 〈自動詞＋前置詞＋動名詞〉という連なりが存在する文。⑧では動名詞に意味上の主語である my が加わっているので，「私が」という情報を確実にとらえる。

■ ⑨⑩⑪ 〈形容詞＋前置詞＋動名詞〉という連なりが存在する文。⑩の my students' は意味上の主語。「私の生徒たちが」と訳す。⑪は形容詞の前の動詞が get（〜になる）なので，get 以下は「〜することに興味を持った状態になる→〜することに興味をもつ（ようになる）」という意味になる。

■ ⑫⑬ 〈群前置詞＋動名詞〉という連なりが存在する文。

 Exercises

次の文を指定された語数で英訳しましょう。（　　　　　）内で示されている語は必要に応じて，形を変えたうえで用いてください。

① 彼女は雑誌を読むことによって自分の英語力を向上させた。（7 語）

....

② 彼は何も言わないでその部屋を出ていった。（7 語）

....

③ 自分の部屋を掃除した後，私はシャワーを浴びた。（8 語）

....

④ 君はアルコールを飲むことを慎まなければならない。（6 語／ refrain）

....

⑤ 私は一人で食事をすることに慣れている。（6 語）

....

⑥ 私たちは家を買う代わりにアパートを借りた。(9語)

....

⑦ 彼女は生命を失う危険があった。(8語／danger)

....

⑧ 彼らはついにそのライオンを捕獲することに成功した。(7語／finally, catch)

....

⑨ 私はこの街に住んでいることに誇りを持っている。(8語／of)

....

⑩ この製品を使用する前に，どうぞこのマニュアルをお読みください。(8語／use)

....

Express English Effectively!

英会話に強くなる英文法・英作文

編著者	マーク・ピーターセン
	澤　井　康　佑
発行者	山　口　隆　史

発　行　所　　　^{株式会社} 音羽書房鶴見書店

〒113-0033　東京都文京区本郷 3-26-13
TEL 03-3814-0491
FAX 03-3814-9250
URL: https://www.otowatsurumi.com
e-mail: info@otowatsurumi.com

2024 年 3 月 1 日　　初版発行

組版　ほんのしろ
装幀　謝　暄慧（オセロ）
印刷・製本　シナノ パブリッシング プレス
■ 落丁・乱丁本はお取り替えいたします。　　　EC-076